NEW STUDIES IN ETHICS

KANT'S MORAL PHILOSOPHY

Kant's Moral Philosophy

H. B. ACTON
Professor of Moral Philosophy, University of Edinburgh

MACMILLAN
ST MARTIN'S PRESS

© H. B. Acton 1970

First published 1970 by
MACMILLAN AND CO LTD
Little Essex Street London W C 2
and also at Bombay Calcutta and Madras
Macmillan South Africa (Publishers) Pty Ltd Johannesburg
The Macmillan Company of Australia Pty Ltd Melbourne
The Macmillan Company of Canada Ltd Toronto
St Martin's Press Inc New York
Gill and Macmillan Ltd Dublin

Library of Congress catalog card no. 71–108405

Printed in Great Britain by
RICHARD CLAY (THE CHAUCER PRESS) LTD
Bungay, Suffolk

CONTENTS

EDITOR'S PREFACE

Kant's fame extends to almost every branch of philosophy and is by no means least in that part of the discipline which has to do with moral discourse. Everyone knows that Kant spoke of moral obligation as a categorical imperative; but what precisely did he mean by this description and what reasons had he for using it? Again, Kant's belief that our moral experience constitutes some kind of proof of God, freedom and immortality is well known; but just what kind of proof was it in Kant's opinion and was that opinion well founded? Professor Acton sheds light on these and other important questions in his admirably clear, concise and comprehensive survey of Kant's moral philosophy.

In this study Kant's ideas about ethics are related to those of other thinkers in his day, both as to their derivation and as to their influence. Professor Acton then expounds Kant's ethics against the background of his philosophy as a whole. He also comments critically upon Kant's ideas and arguments from a standpoint influenced by modern analytical philosophy.

This monograph will be of great help to students and considerable interest to professional philosophers. It will also provide a wider public with an introduction to Kant's formidable writings which is at once scholarly and easy to read.

University of Exeter   W. D. HUDSON

I. INTRODUCTION: KANT AND THE ENLIGHTENMENT

Immanuel Kant was born in Königsberg in East Prussia (now Kaliningrad in the U.S.S.R.) in 1724, and died in the same town in 1804, having taught philosophy in the university there from 1755. With the publication of his *Critique of Pure Reason* in 1781 he became the founder and head of a new school of philosophy, the so-called Critical Philosophy, which was quickly accepted in universities all over Germany and soon gave Kant himself an international reputation. The *Critique of Practical Reason* (1788) and the *Critique of Judgment* (1790) completed Kant's systematic exposition of his views, but both before he wrote the *Critique of Pure Reason* and afterwards, he published voluminously in books and in the press. Furthermore, he lectured on a wide range of topics, including mathematics, physics, cosmology, anthropology (i.e. what today is called psychology), physical geography and education, as well as on natural theology and the various branches of philosophy. His lectures were witty and learned, and people went to Königsberg from all over Germany in order to hear them.

Kant lived, taught and wrote in the course of that intellectual movement known as the Enlightenment. This may be said to have started towards the end of the seventeenth century with writings that called for religious toleration and raised doubts about some of the dogmas of the Christian religion. In the eighteenth century the authority of the churches came under attack, and fundamental questions were raised about the nature of government and its justification. In France Voltaire and Diderot criticised the ideas and practices of the ruling authorities in Church and State, and encouraged people to agree with Bacon and Locke that human knowledge is based on experience, and is to be pursued not for its own sake but for the human happiness it can show the means to. Such writers as d'Holbach and Helvétius reinterpreted morality in hedonistic terms as consisting in rules to be followed with a view to individual happiness. In Germany, however, the Enlightenment took a somewhat different course. The leading German philosopher of the first half of the eighteenth century was Christian Wolff (1679–1754), who elaborated and systematised the work of the great mathematician, logician and philosopher, Leibniz. Now Leibniz had criticised the empiricist elements in Locke's philosophy, that is, the doctrine that all human knowledge of the world is based on sense experience. 'Everything that is in the intellect,' said Leibniz, 'comes from the senses – except the intellect itself.' Wolff, too, adopted this so-called rationalist standpoint. He claimed, as had St Anselm, Descartes and Leibniz before him, that the existence of God can be proved *a priori*, i.e. can be demonstrated on the basis of propositions that are known to be true independently of sense experience. Wolff also held that the basic principles of morality are known *a priori* and independently of divine revelation. According to Wolff, the fundamental rational principle of morality is: 'Do whatever makes you and your own condition and that of all your fellow men more perfect.' Wolff accepted the Stoic view that perfection is achieved by acting in accordance with nature, and that happiness results from doing this but is not itself the aim of moral action.

Wolff was forced by Frederick William I of Prussia to give up his chair of philosophy at Halle in 1723 because of complaints about his teachings by Pietists, whose influence was considerable at that university. Pietism was a movement that had grown up within the Lutheran church in Germany in the previous century. Adherents of this sect set little store by orthodox theology, but encouraged the study of the Bible, the participation of the laity in church affairs and personal involvement in spontaneous devotion and good works. Wolff was suspect to some of his Pietist colleagues because his account of the natural world seemed to leave no room for miracles or for free choice. When Frederick the Great, who admired the leading thinkers of the Enlightenment, came to the throne of Prussia in 1740 he reinstated Wolff at Halle.

Kant came under the influence both of Wolff and of the Pietism that Wolff had fallen foul of. As a boy, Kant went to a school at

Königsberg, where the Director was a Pietist who encouraged the practice of frequent 'spontaneous' prayers, and Kant's teacher at the university of Königsberg when he became a student there in 1740 was Martin Knutzen (1713–51), who somehow contrived to be both a Pietist and a follower of Wolff. Kant was affected by Pietism in two ways. On the one hand, he came to dislike church-going and to regard prayers as either unnecessary, since God already knows our needs, or as conducive to an objectionable form of self-abasement.[1] On the other hand, the Pietist belief that religious conduct is more important than theological orthodoxy remained with him all his life, and later found expression in his view that belief in God, in freedom of the will and in the immortality of the soul cannot be proved on *theoretical* grounds but are postulates of the *practical* reason involved in our duty to obey the moral law.[2]

In the earlier years of his teaching career Kant was a follower of Wolff. In 1762 he published *On the only Possible Demonstrative Proof of the Existence of God*, in which he endeavoured to show that if it is *possible* that God exists, and it *is* possible, then God *must* exist. This, Kant said, is a more thoroughly *a priori* proof than any other, since it does not assume that anything actually exists, and hence makes no use of any empirical premise whatsoever. In an essay written about the same time and published in 1764, the *Enquiry into the Distinctness of the Fundamental Propositions of Natural Theology and Morality*, Kant accepted Wolff's fundamental ethical principle in the form: 'Do the most perfect deed that you can', but he also made a distinction, later to become fundamental to his own moral philosophy, between being obliged to do something as a means to something else that one wants to achieve, and being obliged to do something 'immediately', that is, not merely as a means to something else. It is interesting to notice that in this essay Kant shows appreciation for the ethical writings of Shaftesbury, Hutcheson and Hume, writers who had emphasised feeling and the moral sense rather than reason in morality. This shows that Kant was already extending his view from the German rationalistic form of the Enlightenment to the more empiricist theories being developed elsewhere.

In the Preface to the first edition of the *Critique of Pure Reason* Kant wrote: 'Our age is essentially an age of criticism, to which everything has to submit. Religion, on account of its sanctity, and legislation on account of its majesty, both try to withdraw themselves from it. But they then straightway arouse just suspicion against themselves and cannot claim that sincere respect which reason grants to whoever has been able to withstand its free and open examination.'[3] Kant believed that the function of philosophy in an age of criticism is to subject human reason itself to critical examination. It followed from this that the basis of mathematical and physical knowledge should be enquired into, and that reason should turn its scrutiny upon itself in order to discover its scope and limitations. This is the task that Kant undertook in the *Critique of Pure Reason*.

II. SOME ETHICAL BEARINGS OF KANT'S *CRITIQUE OF PURE REASON*

At the begining of the *Critique of Pure Reason* Kant asks why it is that human knowledge makes continual progress in mathematics and in physics, and yet in metaphysics, the study of God, the freedom of the will, and the nature and destiny of the soul, subjects of great interest to everyone, it is engaged in controversies that seem to go on endlessly without decision. Now Wolff had claimed to give definite answers to these questions, so it is clear that Kant no longer believed that Wolff's metaphysics is adequate. Kant says that he had been aroused from his 'dogmatic slumber'[4] by David Hume. It is possible that Kant came to appreciate the empiricist view that human knowledge is based on sense experience and cannot go beyond it as a result of reading Sulzer's German translation of Hume's *Enquiry concerning Human Understanding*, in which the Scottish philosopher had said that books of metaphysics can contain 'nothing but sophistry and illusion'. A similar conclusion as to the fruitlessness of metaphysics had been reached by the French philosopher Condillac (1715–80) in his *Traité des Systèmes* (1749).

Kant, then, recognised that there was a great contrast between the dogmatic metaphysics of Wolff and the plausibly argued empiricist anti-metaphysical view of Hume. Kant, like many others at that time and since, was impressed by Hume's contention that our belief that every event must have a cause has no rational justification but is a habit of expectation resulting from the constant association of experiences in the past. But although Kant was impressed by this view, he did not feel able to accept it, since he thought that it implied that the causal laws established in the natural sciences do not describe objective sequences in nature but indicate merely subjective experiences in the minds of men. Kant

5

concluded, therefore, that when empiricism is consistent and complete it gives rise to scepticism, and hence becomes incompatible with the unassailable objectivity of scientific knowledge generally. Nevertheless, Kant believed that the empiricists were right to emphasise that sense experience is essential to human knowledge. In the part of the *Critique of Pure Reason* called the Transcendental Dialectic Kant showed that by using *a priori* arguments uncontrolled by empirical reference it is possible to prove contradictory conclusions. It could be argued, for example, both that the world must have a beginning in time and that it cannot, both that there must be uncaused freedom of the will and that such freedom is impossible and everything whatsoever occurs according to the laws of nature. Since two contradictory propositions cannot both be true, there must be something defective or incomplete in forms of argument that appear to prove both of them. Kant's view is that principles like 'every event has a cause' are formal principles which bring order and intelligibility to our sense impressions but have no objective significance apart from them.

Kant gave the names 'pure concepts of the understanding' and 'categories' to these formal principles which we employ to interpret sense impressions which, without them, would present only a meaningless confusion. He chose the term 'categories' because Aristotle had used this word for the most general forms of thing, he called them 'pure' because, unlike concepts such as 'house', they are not formed from what is observed in experience, and he said they are concepts of 'the understanding' because it is the intellect that brings order into our sense impressions by thinking of them in terms of these principles. According to Kant, the reason why nature appears as a world of interacting things obeying causal laws is that we can only interpret our sense impressions by organising them in terms of the categories of substance, cause and reciprocity.

Kant drew certain negative conclusions from this, not unlike those of Hume and of nineteenth- and twentieth-century positivists. Since *a priori* argumentation about God, freedom and the soul is in principle fruitless, metaphysics, in the sense of a rationally argued account of how the world must be, has to be rejected.

There is only one way to find out about the world, and that is by investigating it with the experimental methods of the natural sciences. Human beings are parts of nature, and since we must think of nature as a system of causally connected things, human beings are subject to causal determination like everything else. As parts of the natural world, men are determined, not free, and, like flies and fish, they die and are seen and heard no more.

But the *Critique of Pure Reason* is not entirely negative. Kant argued that the deterministic world revealed by the natural sciences is the world *as it appears* to beings who have to perceive by the senses. We are not justified in assuming, however, that the world as it appears to men is identical with the world *as it is in itself*. For one thing the understanding actively interprets ('synthesises') the sense impressions it passively receives, and this enables us to conceive the possibility of spontaneous, uncaused activity, even though we cannot scientifically investigate it. We do not know how the passive sense impressions come into being, and there may be some super-sensible world of things-in-themselves responsible for them. Furthermore, we can conceive of the possibility of noumena which the understanding can apprehend without having to receive sense impressions, and these noumena might be spontaneously active beings not subject to causal necessity. Neither God nor immaterial souls are *known* by us scientifically, but they are possibilities. We cannot have *theoretical* knowledge *of* them, but there might be *practical* reasons for believing *in* them.

This brings us to Kant's view that the reason is practical as well as theoretical. If we regard men as concerned only to satisfy their natural desires and to secure happiness thereby, their reason would have merely the subordinate theoretical function of discovering the means by which happiness may be secured, and since different people want different things, these means will vary from one individual to another. But men are not satisfied merely to be happy, but want to *deserve* to be happy, and consider themselves subject to a moral law that is independent of the desires their experience shows them to have. Kant writes:

I assume that there really exist pure moral laws which entirely *a priori* (without regard to empirical notions, i.e. happiness) determine the acts and omissions i.e. the use of the freedom of any rational being, and that these laws command absolutely (not only hypothetically, on the presupposition of other hypothetical ends) and are therefore absolutely necessary. I can justifiably assume this by appealing not only to the proofs of the most enlightened moralists, but also to the moral judgment of every man, if only he tries to think a law of that sort clearly.[5]

Kant is here saying that when rational beings consider what they ought to do, their practical reason commands them to act independently of any particular desires or aims they in fact have. Scientific laws are discovered by examining the natural world for causal sequences. Men do not, however, discover their duty by such theoretical procedures, but by recognising the categorical requirements of practical reason. The moral law is 'pure', that is, it contains no notions based on experience of how things are, like 'it is imprudent to be absent-minded' – some absent-minded people, indeed, do very well – and it is *a priori*, that is, it is not derived from our experience of what tends to make us happy or unhappy. It will be noticed that Kant here expresses with greater precision the distinction he drew in his *Enquiry into the Distinctness of the Fundamental Propositions of Natural Theology and Morality* between being obliged to do something as a means to something else and being obliged to do something 'immediately'.

III. KANT'S DISCUSSION OF THE ORDINARY MORAL CONSCIOUSNESS

We have just seen that in the *Critique of Pure Reason* Kant said that his view about *a priori* moral laws which 'command absolutely' is also the view of 'every man, if only he tries to think a law of that sort clearly'. In the *Groundwork of the Metaphysic of Morals* (1785) – hereafter to be called the *Groundwork* – Kant showed that he was in earnest in thus referring to the moral beliefs of ordinary men, for he devotes the first section of the book to an analysis and defence of them, referring to 'the common reason of mankind'[6] and 'the ordinary moral rational knowledge'.[7] It might be thought most unlikely that ordinary men could believe, even implicitly, anything so complex and technical as that the moral law is *a priori* and pure, that is, that it is known independently of experience and contains in itself no concepts that are derived from experience. Yet this is just what Kant seeks to show.

Kant's conception of the function of reason in morality is undoubtedly influenced by his conception of the categories in making human knowledge possible. Nevertheless, if he really means to assert that his view of rational morality is presupposed in the ordinary morality of rational men, arguments based on the philosophical conclusions of the *Critique of Pure Reason* are not essential. Indeed, he himself points out that there is an important difference between the theoretical and the practical reason. To employ pure *a priori* concepts without reference to sense experience is to run into all the difficulties and contradictions described in the Transcendental Dialectic, whereas in morality the practical reason has to be kept free from 'all sensuous motives',[8] and is *led astray* when it falls in with them.

According to Kant, it is possible to act from one or a combination of three sorts of motive: from the motive of complying with the *a priori* command of reason expressed in the moral law; from the motive of satisfying as many desires as possible so as to get the greatest possible happiness for oneself; or from completely irrational desire or inclination. According to Kant, only the first sort of motive is wholly rational. There is something rational in seeking one's own happiness, for the seeker after happiness has to form an idea of his happiness as a whole and has to discover what means conduce to it. Kant thinks that the imagination is involved in forming an idea of one's happiness as a whole and that the discovering of means for achieving happiness entails empirical enquiry leading to knowledge that is not *a priori*. To be moved by love or hate for someone is, in Kant's terminology, to be moved by 'inclination', and this is not rational at all.

The contrast between obeying the *a priori* command of the moral law and seeking one's own happiness corresponds fairly well with the ordinary distinction between duty and personal interest. Everyone agrees that although it is not in itself wrong to seek one's own happiness, a man who seeks nothing but this and does not try to do his duty is rightly an object of moral disapproval. Kant argued that men could conceivably have been so constituted that instinct rather than reason led to their preservation and welfare.[9] The fact that they have not been so constituted suggested to Kant that reason has some other function in men than that of being, as Hume had said it was, 'the slave of the passions'. Kant believed, furthermore, that there is an important *logical* difference between such a precept as 'Thou shalt not lie' and prudential, happiness-securing precepts, such as 'Honesty is the best policy'. According to Kant, 'Thou shalt not lie' is a universal and rational command that would be binding on rational beings other than men, if there were such.[10] 'Honesty is the best policy', on the other hand, may *generally* lead to the happiness of those who adopt it,[11] men and their circumstances being what they are, but occasions may arise when departure from the precept might bring still more happiness. Just as the laws of logic are not discovered by observation and experiment but are recognised to be necessarily true, so, according to Kant, the laws of morality are necessarily valid, whereas rules for obtaining happiness could have been different from what they are had men and the world been different. It is interesting to notice that G. E. Moore, in *Principia Ethica* (1903), argued that since such principles as 'Thou shalt not lie', or even 'Thou shalt not commit murder' are dependent upon statements about what generally produces good results, they cannot be necessarily and universally valid, but only generally acceptable.[12] Kant argues, on the contrary, that these principles cannot depend on statements about what generally produces happiness just because they are necessarily and universally valid.

There is no doubt that people generally believe that, just as what Kant calls obedience to the moral law and what is more often called doing what is right takes precedence over merely personal interest, so it takes precedence over satisfying particular desires or inclinations. It would not be generally believed, for example, that someone is justified in telling a lie merely because by so doing he can injure someone whom he hates. It may be suggested, however, that behaviour motivated by love for individuals should take precedence over following moral rules or acting with a view to doing one's duty. Indeed, adherents of what is today called Situational Ethics do maintain that spontaneous love is superior to the following of moral rules. The outlook expressed in the Sermon on the Mount, they say, is far superior to the rule-bound moralism of the Pharisees. Love is above the moral law, it is said, and raises human action to its highest level. Kant does not say that action inspired by spontaneous love or sympathetic feeling has no value at all, but he does not think it has moral value. According to Kant, morality involves answering to the call of duty, and nothing can be our duty which we are unable to do. But, he holds, feelings of love and sympathy may come and go irrespective of our will, and cannot be summoned up to order. In the *Groundwork* Kant uses the expression 'pathological love' for love or sympathy understood as an 'inclination'. He does not use the adjective 'pathological' in the twentieth-century sense of 'diseased', but in its earlier sense of 'of the nature of feeling', in accordance with the meaning of the Greek word *pathos*. The love commanded by Jesus when he said that we should love one another and love our enemies could not, according to Kant, be

B

the love of feeling or sympathy, for it is not in our power to summon this up at will. What we can do is to help one another, and try to help even our enemies. 'Melting compassion'[13] cannot be required of us, but the 'love of mankind'[14] can arise after we have engaged in acts of beneficence. The duty of beneficence, on Kant's view, is not a matter of feeling but is carried out under the guidance of the rational will. His position is made clear in the following passage from the *Critique of Practical Reason*:

> Inclination is blind and slavish whether it be of a good sort or not, and when morality is in question, reason must not play the part merely of guardian to inclination, but, disregarding it altogether, must attend simply to its own interest as pure practical reason. This very feeling of compassion and softhearted sympathy, if it precedes deliberation on what our duty is, and becomes a determining principle, is even annoying to right-thinking persons, brings their deliberate maxims into confusion, and makes them wish to be delivered from it and to be subject to law-giving reason alone.[15]

According to Kant's terminology, someone who acts in order to fulfil the moral law acts from 'good will' or 'from duty'. Action from self-love may be good or may be bad, according as the consequences are good or bad, and so may action resulting from love as a mere inclination. But action from 'good will', according to Kant, is always good and can never be bad, and is therefore 'good without qualification' or 'unreservedly good'. An action prompted and guided by the rational moral will, with the intention of performing a duty, of doing what is right, retains its value as a moral action even if it turns out badly as a result of some unhappy chance beyond the agent's control. It follows from this that an action does not derive its moral value from the results it succeeds in bringing about, but from 'the maxim', as Kant calls it, that is, from the type of willed action intended by the agent. Kant therefore believes that morally good actions are those with morally good intentions, and that actions with morally good intentions are actions carried out 'from duty'. Such actions, he says, have an 'inner worth'.[16]

We may now ask whether Kant is right in thinking that the ordinary moral consciousness takes this view. It does seem true that as civilisation has developed, more and more emphasis has been placed upon the motives and intentions of action and less upon the mere fact of what was actually done. Among uncivilised peoples men are condemned and punished for what civilised men call accidents, i.e. for things that people did not do intentionally. Among civilised men a 'guilty mind' or 'guilty intent' (*mens rea*) is considered a prerequisite for just legal condemnation. If this is so in the legal sphere it is still more obvious in the less institutionally regulated circumstances of the moral life, where people's actions come to be regarded as revelations of themselves as well as interferences in the course of things. Kant is therefore right in so far as he is saying that among civilised men the moral value of an action depends upon the intention which it expresses rather than upon what eventuates when a well-intentioned or evilly intentioned action is actually performed.

But Kant goes beyond this, and says that the good will that ordinary men morally approve is the rational will, the pure *a priori* practical reason. It is much less obvious that ordinary men accept or could be brought to accept this part of Kant's view. They probably do agree that self-interested action, although not always or even generally bad, is inferior morally to action done 'from duty'. But they might be less inclined to agree with him that action springing from 'pathological love' is morally inferior to action done 'from duty'. Many men, especially those who live in liberal societies, are sentimental and tend to value 'sympathy' and 'compassion' very highly and to regard them as moral feelings. Still, on reflection they may come to distinguish, as Professor Paton does, between 'the man who is good and the man who is good-natured or good-hearted'.[17] Even the empiricist Hume, who held that morality is fundamentally a matter of feeling, recognised that not any and every sort of sympathetic feeling is a moral feeling, but that in making moral judgments we adopt a disinterested point of view and try to view our own actions as a disinterested observer might view them. In the light of such considerations, then, the ordinary man might recognise that there is something rational about moral motives that distinguishes them at any rate from cruder forms of love and sympathy as well as from self-interest. But it is doubtful whether he would go all the way with Kant and say that moral motives are based upon a pure and *a priori* practical reason. This appears to be a point at which Kant's view goes beyond anything that is considered in the ordinary man's morality. We shall have to discuss this later.

Although Kant considers that morality is basically rational, he agrees with empiricist philosophers and with ordinary men that there is an element of feeling or emotion in it too. He identifies the moral feeling or emotion with what he calls reverence or respect (*Achtung*), a feeling which only a rational being aware of the moral law can have. Reverence is quite different from the feeling someone has when he contemplates an individual who is beautiful, clever, powerful or successful. He can admire such people, but admiration is not 'awareness of a rule that abolishes my self-love'[18] as reverence for the moral law does. Reverence, according to Kant, is analogous to fear, in that it is felt by relation to *the command* of the moral law, and it is analogous to inclination in that it is '*self-produced* through a concept of reason'. But although this moral feeling is produced by reason, it could not be experienced by beings who did not also have irrational inclinations and desires. For the reverence which involves the abolition of my self-love is only felt when I compare my own irrational sense-given inclinations with the possibility of acting for the sake of the moral law. Kant writes:

Reverence applies always to persons only, never to things. The latter may arouse *inclination* in us, and if they are animals (e.g. horses, dogs, etc.) even *love* or *fear*, like the sea, a volcano, a beast of prey, but never *reverence* ... a man may also be an object to me of love, fear, or admiration even to the extent of astonishment, and yet not be an object of reverence ... Fontenelle says: 'I bow before an outstanding man, but my mind does not bow'. I would add, before an unimportant ordinary man in whom I perceive uprightness of character in a higher degree than I am conscious of in myself, *my mind does bow*, whether or not I want to do so, however high I may bear my head so that he shall not overlook my superior rank. Why is this? Because his example exhibits to me a law that humbles my self-conceit when I compare it with my conduct; a law the *practicability* of obedience to which I see proved by the deed before my eyes.[19]

Whether or not Kant has here described the moral feeling that is essential to morality, he seems to have gone somewhat beyond the ordinary morality when he says in the *Groundwork* that if one is to have a morally good will in acting one must ask: 'Can you also will that the maxim of your action become a universal law?'[20] Kant explains this in terms of the following example. Could a man will that making a lying promise for his own advantage should become a universal practice? Kant says that you cannot, for if everyone lied, no one would make a promise, and so the law would 'destroy itself'. This, he says, is 'the first principle' of the 'moral knowledge of ordinary human reason', and he goes on to claim that 'with this compass in hand' it is possible to distinguish good from evil and right from wrong, and that hence 'there is no need of science and philosophy for knowing what a man has to do in order to be honest and good',[21] I am inclined to say that the ordinary man would not know how to make use of this compass. He would, therefore, need instruction, and would presumably turn to a moral philosopher to provide it. We must therefore move on from the ordinary moral consciousness into the field of philosophical discussion in order to discover the nature and powers of the compass that Kant offers to us.

IV. HYPOTHETICAL IMPERATIVES AND THE CATEGORICAL IMPERATIVE

In section I above we noted that in an early essay Kant had distinguished between being obliged to do something as a means to something else and being obliged 'immediately'. In section II we quoted a passage from the *Critique of Pure Reason* in which Kant says that moral laws 'command absolutely (not only hypothetically on the presupposition of other empirical ends)'. In section III we considered his distinction between acting from inclination or with a view to happiness on the one hand, and acting 'from duty' on the other, and we noticed his view that an individual can find out whether he is acting from duty by asking himself: 'Can I also will that the maxim of my action become a universal law?' The idea that Kant has been working towards in these passages is that of the Categorical Imperative. He explains it in section II of the *Groundwork* and in book I, chapter I of the *Critique of Practical Reason*.

What Kant says about the categorical imperative is closely linked with his account of acting 'from duty', and so, by contrast, with his accounts of acting from inclination and with a view to individual happiness. We can see how this link is made if we consider the notion of 'ought', which can be used both in the context of duty and in the context of inclination and happiness. The notion of 'ought' is of use for beings like men who are rational and yet have inclinations and desires which might conflict with what reason requires. Animals whose actions are determined entirely by desires and inclinations would have no use for the notion, but would just react to the strongest urge. God, on the other hand, or, as Kant puts it, 'a holy will'[22] or 'the head' of the Kingdom of Ends,[23] has a conception of the moral law but no inclination to go against it, and so has no use for the expression 'I ought' or for the notion of duty as applied to himself. Men come between God and the animals, so that when their inclinations are against it, what is rational seems like something imposed on them from outside which 'necessitates' or forces them. It is in this way that Kant comes to regard rules of action as imperatives. He writes:

> The conception of an objective principle, so far as it is necessitating for a will is called a command (of reason), and the formula of this command is called an *imperative*.
>
> All imperatives are expressed by an 'ought', and by this they mark the relation of an objective law of reason to a will which is not necessarily determined by it (a necessitation).[24]

It helps us to understand this word 'necessitation' if we realise that it is used by Kant by relation to a rule or law that might be resisted, and that it is used to mean 'to oblige', 'to force', 'to compel' or 'to press', as when, for example, a visitor is pressed to stay. Abbott, in his version of the passage quoted above translates what I (following Paton) have translated by 'it is necessitating for a will' and by 'a necessitation', by 'it is obligatory for a will' and by 'an obligation'. It will be realised that obliging someone to do something is often equivalent to making him do it or forcing him to do it, and it is Kant's view that a being who can use the expression 'I ought' must have this notion of being obliged or forced when he uses it.

Now let us consider what Kant has to say about what he calls hypothetical imperatives. These comprise those 'oughts' or 'obligations' or 'necessitations' that are not duties and are not moral. Kant distinguished two sorts of hypothetical imperatives which he calls, respectively, Rules of Skill and Counsels (or Recommendations) of Prudence.

Rules of Skill he explains as follows. A doctor who wants to cure his patient and knows how to do so has in his mind such rules as 'administer such and such a drug for jaundice', 'keep the patient warm for treating shock' and so on. But someone who wants to kill the patient might have in mind such rules as 'administer so many grains of arsenic' or 'let the patient get cold'. What the doctor or the poisoner is obliged to do, forced to do, necessitated to do, depends upon the end he wishes to bring about.

Once he has chosen his end, his course is settled objectively by the means in fact necessary for achieving the end. (The word that Kant uses for 'necessary' here is *notwendig*, a different word and notion from necessitation (*Nötigung*) above.) The doctor who knows how to treat his patient may be deflected from his course by laziness, the poisoner who knows how to kill may be deflected from his course by fear of being caught. As the one gets lazy and the other begins to feel nervous, the former may say 'if I am to bring about a cure, I ought to . . .', and the latter 'if I am to kill him I ought to . . .', and they would fill in the necessary means according to their knowledge of what produces the end they are seeking, according to their knowledge of 'the objective laws of reason'. Kant points out that a large part of our education consists in acquiring skills for doing things we might or might not have occasion to do. Whether we use these skills depends upon what we choose to do, and many of our choices are arbitrary. The imperatives involved in Rules of Skill Kant calls 'problematic' just because the ends they are meant to secure are ends that we might or might not pursue.

Counsels of Prudence he explains in the following way. Everyone wants to be happy, and everyone learns rules that are meant to help him to become so. We are told to look after our health, to be moderate in all things, to be reasonably sociable and so on. Each man's happiness consists in as full and harmonious a fulfilment of his desires as can be obtained. People's wants and wishes differ and change from time to time, so that knowledge of what makes them happy is less stable and definite than knowledge of what kills and cures. Even so, people can be tempted away from doing what is likely to promote their happiness as a whole, and then they may find themselves thinking: 'I ought to limit my drinking' or 'I ought to work harder'. We can each of us learn what we have to do to keep happy, and although the means to happiness may differ from one person to another, what they are can often be objectively established. Kant takes it that everyone would like to be happy, and would therefore do what would make him happy if he knew how to. There is nothing problematic about the search for happiness as there is about the exercise of a skill which only interests some people sometimes. Hence Kant says that Counsels of Prudence are expressed in principles that are assertoric. Rules of Skill are problematic because they might or might not be exercised, and Counsels of Prudence are assertoric because everyone in fact pursues the end they are fitted to secure.

We saw in section III that the pursuit of one's own happiness might bring one into conflict with morality, and that in this conflict morality ought to prevail. No Rule of Skill need concern a man who does not seek the end that it prescribes the means to. 'Castor oil purges' is an objective generalisation discovered by the theoretical reason and utilised by a doctor who wants to cure a patient. (It was also used in Nazi Germany to cause distress to Jews.) 'Be thrifty when you are young' is a Counsel of Prudence which does not have to be followed by men who do not see their happiness in a comfortable old age. 'Do not make deceitful promises' is independent of personal aims and idiosyncratic views of happiness. It is independent, therefore, of theoretical knowledge of how the world is, but is objectively valid for all men whatever they may wish or want. Kant says – as he had said in 1764 – that it enjoins 'immediately' and is apodeictic, that is, is absolute and allows none of the qualifications that problematic and assertoric judgments do.[25] No rational being can escape its authority by claiming that it is not meant for people with his peculiar wants and tastes.

Three comments are called for at this stage of our exposition:

(1) Professor L. W. Beck has pointed out[26] that it is not the hypothetical or categorical *form* of imperatives that is essential to Kant's view, for non-moral imperatives ('Shut the door') can be expressed in categorical form, and moral imperatives ('If you promised to return the book, do so') can be expressed in hypothetical form. What is essential is the absoluteness of a principle that is valid for everyone, whoever he may be.

(2) It is important to notice Kant's use of the term 'objective' in the present context. He is using it in contrast with the 'subjective' character of Rules of Skill and Counsels of Prudence. These are subjective in the sense that their nature and their authority varies from one person to another and even from one time to

another in a person's life. As tastes and aims vary with time and circumstance, rules of conduct that were once compelling are abandoned and replaced by others. The moral law is not like that. It applies to everyone, everywhere and always.

(3) According to Kant, then, Rules of Skill and Counsels of Prudence gain their obligatory force from men's aims and dispositions and the nature of the world in which they find themselves. The apodeictic moral law, he therefore thought, must be independent of all these things and be both *a priori* and pure. It could not therefore be directly concerned with actions which have to be described in empirical terms, such as telling the truth or promising, which involve saying and doing things in the natural world. Kant concluded that the philosopher must seek for an aspect of actions which is more fundamental than their manifestation in nature, and that this must consist in 'the purely formal laws' of the will.[27] This is difficult to understand, but at least one thing is clear. When he explains the notion of the Categorical Imperative Kant gives examples of such moral rules of action as not making lying promises. But Kant's main concern was to elicit the rational principle of willing which he believed lay behind all the specific moral rules for action in the world. Just as in the Old and New Testaments 'the Law' means the whole body of Jewish law, so 'the moral law' can mean the whole body of moral rules and principles. But the expression 'the moral law' suggested to Kant the idea of a single supreme principle governing all the specific rules of morality. When Jesus said that the whole of the law and the prophets consists in loving God and one's neighbour he was calling attention to the principles animating the complexities of the Jewish legislation. Similarly, Kant believed that there is a supreme principle of morality which informs all the particular moral rules but does not itself refer to any specific types of action. We must now see what he has to say about this.

V. THE SUPREME PRINCIPLE OF MORALITY: UNIVERSAL LAW

Kant states the supreme formal principle of the will in the following terms: '*Act only on that maxim through which you can at the same time will that it should become a universal law.*'[28] A maxim, Kant says, is 'a subjective principle of action'.[29] By this he means a rule of action a man follows as part of his own policy of living, whatever rules of living other people may have. Maxims are contrasted by Kant with laws, which are objectively valid for all rational beings A maxim is *mine* or *his*, a law applies to *everyone*. A man may make an objective law his own subjective maxim by deciding that he will always follow it. The principle we have just quoted, then, means that people should only adopt as rules of living for themselves rules that they can will should be always followed by everyone.

We have already seen that Kant regarded this as a formal principle of the will and not as a material principle of action depending upon empirical aims and desires. We may notice, too, that Kant states his law by relation to the maxims that men might adopt, and hence is regarding it as limiting the maxims according to which it is permissible for men to act. Maxims that cannot pass the test of universalisation are ruled out, but it is not said that every conceivably universalised maxim is part of the moral law. From the fact that everyone could adopt the maxim of touching his head at least once a day it does not follow that there is a moral duty to do so. What Kant tries to show is that maxims that go against moral principles cannot be universalised.

Kant tries to support this fundamental principle by applying it to a number of instances in a systematic way. He divides duties into those owed to oneself and those owed to others, and then into perfect and imperfect duties to oneself and to others. Kant's account of this latter distinction is not altogether clear, but he regards perfect duties as those which call for a specific act of fulfilment as with keeping a promise, which requires the promisor to perform some specific act which is the keeping of the promise. Imperfect duties allow latitude in the manner of their performance, as with the duty to help others, which does not call for any particular act. A man might fulfil his duty to help others by helping this man or that man at one time or at another time. Kant also regards perfect duties as duties which cannot be overridden and imperfect duties as capable of being overridden, as happens when a duty to help A is overridden by a more pressing duty to help B.[30] Assuming this classification, then, Kant in the *Groundwork* tests out his principle of universal law by reference to suicide (i.e. going against the perfect duty to oneself to preserve one's life), to laziness and self-indulgence (i.e. going against the imperfect duty to oneself to cultivate one's talents), to lying promises (i.e. going against the perfect duty to others to keep promises) and to the refusal to help others (i.e. going against the imperfect duty of beneficence to others). In the *Critique of Practical Reason* Kant supports his principle of universal law by reference to someone who keeps a deposit that has been left with him (i.e. going against the perfect duty to others to return goods or money entrusted to one). There is not enough space for us to consider Kant's treatment of all these cases, and as some people find difficulty in the very notion of a duty owed to oneself, it will be convenient to consider what Kant says about perfect and imperfect duties to others. Let us then examine three of his examples.

(1) A man contemplates borrowing some money that he has no intention of paying back. The maxim of the action which he contemplates is 'Whenever I find myself short of money, I will borrow money and promise to pay it back, though I know this will never be done'. According to Kant this could not become everyone's maxim always, because if everyone did this always 'it would make promising, and the very purpose of promising itself impossible, since no one would believe he was being promised anything, but would laugh at utterances of this kind as empty shams'.[31]

(2) In the *Critique of Pratical Reason* Kant says that if a man con-

templates keeping a deposit left with him for which no receipt was asked or given, he can consider whether 'everyone may deny a deposit of which no one can produce a proof' could become a universal law. It could not, 'because the result would be that there would be no deposits'.[32]

(3) In the *Groundwork* Kant gives the example of a man who does not intend to observe the moral law of beneficence, the principle of helping other people. From what Kant says it appears that this man's maxim would be: 'Not being in distress myself, I do not propose ever to help others.' When this is universalised it becomes: 'Let no one who is not in distress ever give help to anyone else.' According to Kant, if this were adopted, society could continue and there would be no breakdown as promising would break down if everyone made promises with the intention of breaking them, but no one could *will* this to happen, since everyone needs 'love and sympathy' sometimes.[33]

Kant seems to be correct in his analysis of (1). If no one ever intended to keep the promises he made – not merely, as it is now, that many people do not intend to keep their promises – then promising would break down. For promising to take place, at least one promisee must trust one promisor. If from now on no promisor ever intended to keep his promises, then promisees, who also would not intend to keep *their* promises, would not believe what promisors said to them and promises would cease to be made. If, before the institution of promising, no one ever intended to keep a promise, no one would believe a promisor, and promising could never even get started. Promise-breaking makes sense only when some people make promises which they intend to keep.

Sir David Ross does not think that Kant's argument holds, and objects that if every promise is to be broken 'every promise could be relied on to be broken, and this would in many (though not in all) cases serve as well as if it could be relied on to be kept'.[34] This is ingenious, but will not do. 'Rely on' can mean either 'trust' or 'reasonably expect'. If every promisee could *trust* every promisor to break his promise, then this would mean that promising was actually being done, but in the disguise of a code in which things mean their opposites – 'When I say I shall do x, I mean I shall not do x'. This would not be a case of making lying promises. If, on the other hand, a situation arose in which everyone could reasonably expect that all promises would be broken, trust and with it promising would be in process of breaking down, and false promising would not 'serve as well' as honest promising. It has not been sufficiently noticed that Kant does not discuss the breaking of promises but the making of lying promises. The universal making of lying promises is an impossibility. The universal breaking of promises is so too, but this impossibility depends upon the absence of the trust that promising requires.

Kant's example about the deposit is less convincing, perhaps because deposits and receipts are less fundamental in society than promises are. One slip that Kant makes is in supposing that if everyone kept for themselves deposits for which there was no receipt there would be no more deposits. But all he is entitled to say is that there would be *no more deposits without receipts*, for everyone would now demand a receipt before making a deposit, and this might be a good thing for the institution of deposits, as it would make it more effective. What Kant may be presumed to have meant to say, then, is that there could be no system of deposits if everyone kept deposits entrusted to him, and so the universal retention of deposits would 'destroy itself'.

It is against this argument that Hegel brings one of his objections to Kant's position. In an essay entitled *On the Scientific Treatment of Natural Law* (1803), Hegel says that all that Kant's argument shows is that a system without deposits is contradicted by a system with deposits, but not that there is any contradiction in a system without deposits. Kant makes there seem to be a contradiction in a system without deposits because he assumes that everyone would want there to be deposits, and this, says Hegel, shows that Kant was assuming the system of property and was arguing that if everyone kept what belongs to others there could be no system of property. The interesting question, Hegel goes on, just is why there should be property, and about this Kant says nothing. In his *Hegelian Ethics* Professor W. H. Walsh applies this objection to Kant's discussion of lying promises and says that if everyone made lying promises no promises would be made, but that 'it does not follow that a world without promises would be morally inferior to the existing world'. All that Kant shows, therefore, is that it is impossible to retain the institution of promising and at the same always go against what is essential to it.[35]

Kant's position, I suggest, can be defended against this criticism in the following way. His argument about deposits has two aspects. The man who does not pay back the deposit with which he has been entrusted commits an act of theft (which presupposes the institution of property), and a breach of promise, since as guardian of the deposit he must have promised to return it. If promising and property are both of them institutions, promising would appear to be the more fundamental, and even if we grant that human society is conceivable without property, we may well question whether it is conceivable without promising. For would not such a society be one in which no arrangements of any sort could be made which depended upon co-operation between individuals who were not continually in one another's presence? If plans and projects are to be undertaken parts of which have to be carried out by different people at different times and places, they must assure one another that they can each go on with their own part of it, and it is by means of promises that this is done. To this it may be objected that it only pushes the argument a stage farther back, since it may be questioned whether a society without these complicated plans is inferior to one with them. I should say, however, that such a society would be sub-human. Any human society presupposes that everyone ought to trust and be trusted. This line of thought, it seems to me, has some support in Kant's own words. We have seen that Kant says that society could continue even if no one were beneficent – his own words are 'mankind could get on perfectly well'.[36] When he says this he is obviously contrasting universal non-beneficence with universal lying promises, and implying that mankind could not get on if the latter prevailed.

We have seen that Kant thought that the difference between universal promise-breaking and universal non-beneficence is that the latter involves no contradiction and is consistent with the continuance of human society. He argues that no one could *will* universal non-beneficence, and his reason in the *Groundwork* is that the man who universalised the selfish maxim into 'Let no one who is not in distress ever give help to anyone else' would, in so doing, be at the same time willing to rob himself of the love and sympathy which he is bound to want for himself at some time. Schopenhauer, in a famous criticism of Kant, interprets this as an appeal to egoism and writes:

> From this point of view, therefore, my *egoism* decides for justice and philanthropy, not because it desires to *practice* these virtues, but because it wants to *experience* them, rather like the miser who, after listening to a sermon on benevolence exclaimed:
> How superbly given, how fine!
> I should almost like to go begging.[37]

Professor Paton, a much more sympathetic expositor, in his note on Kant's argument, admits that 'it is put in a prudential way',[38] but refers to other passages in the *Groundwork* in which Kant distinguishes between helping others from duty and helping them in order to benefit oneself. But this is no answer to the criticism that in this crucial passage of his argument Kant gives a prudential justification, i.e. a justification based upon the agent's own future happiness, and hence upon a merely hypothetical, assertoric imperative, for a moral principle which he claims is categorical and apodeictic.

Elsewhere [39] Paton refers to a passage in Kant's later *Metaphysic of Morals* (1797) for a more adequate statement of Kant's view.

> It is every man's duty to be beneficent, that is, to promote, according to his means, the happiness of others who are in need, and this without hope of gaining anything by it.
> For every man who finds himself in need wishes to be helped by other men. But if he lets his maxim of not willing to help others in turn when they are in need become public, i.e. makes this a universal permissive law, then everyone would likewise deny him assistance when he needs it, or at least would be entitled to. Hence the maxim of self-interest contradicts itself when it is made universal law – that is, it is contrary to duty. Consequently the maxim of common interest – of beneficence towards the needy – is a universal duty of men, and indeed

for this reason: that men are to be considered fellow-men – that is, rational beings with needs, united by nature in one dwelling-place for the purpose of helping one another.[40]

This is a strange passage. It begins by saying that the moral principle of beneficence is not to be justified on the basis of individual prudence, and then goes on to give what appears to be a prudential reason for it. For the argument that if a man's selfish maxim were universalised he would not obtain help from others appears to give such a reason. But I suggest that we can extract the following theses from it. (a) A man who refuses to help others has no right to any help from them. This accords with that popular form of the Golden Rule according to which help should be reciprocal. (b) Presumably there is a conflict between 'I propose to help nobody' and 'Let nobody help anybody', if the propounder of the first wants to be helped. For nobody can receive help without somebody else giving it. (c) It may be suggested that Kant was not appealing to the egoism of each individual but was saying that *everyone* would lose by universal selfishness. (d) The argument has also been interpreted in terms of kindness[41] – and this has support in Kant's phrase 'love and sympathy' in the *Groundwork*. His argument would then be that if no one were ever kind to anyone without demanding kindness in return no one would be kind at all, since kindness just *is* willingly giving without requiring a return.

Kant did not analyse his view on the law of benevolence in any detail, and we may make it more explicit if we consider various sorts of selfish maxim that might be entertained, and hence the different sorts of law that would result from universalising them.

(i) 'I do not propose to be kind to anyone' when universalised becomes: 'Let no one be kind to anyone.' If to be kind is to help someone for his sake and not for the sake of the helper's advantage this universal law prescribes universal selfishness. It seems to be logically and factually possible, and no contradiction arises from the universalisation of the selfish maxim in this way. It prescribes the state of affairs which some egoistic philosophers have said actually exists.

(ii) 'I only propose to be kind to those who are kind to me' becomes: 'Let no one be kind to anyone except in return for kindness from them.' This is equivalent to saying that no one is to help anyone else for his own sake unless the individual helped helps his helper for his helper's sake. But this is self-contradictory, for to help someone *only* for his sake is inconsistent with helping him in order to get help from him. If A is kind to B only in order that B shall be kind to him A is not being kind but is striking a bargain. 'Love seeketh not her own.'[42] If the selfish maxim is stated and generalised in this way it leads to a contradiction and not, as Kant says, to a mere conflict of the will.

(iii) Let us now consider, not kindness but helping, which is a component in the notion of kindness. Let the maxim be: 'I do not propose to help anyone except with a view to help from others.' When universalised this becomes: 'Let no one help anyone except with a view to receiving help from others.' This is a formula for fairly enlightened self-interest, and recommends a cautious throwing of one's bread upon the waters. Help is not to be given only in immediate exchange for an equivalent but also more widely in the expectation that help will come one's way when it is needed.

(iv) 'I propose to help no one except *in exchange for* help from that one' becomes when universalised: 'Let no one ever help anyone except *in exchange for* help from that one.' This proscribes all gratuitous help and thus envisages a society in which no help is given and all help is bought. From the point of view of their own advantage, people with something to give who think it possible they might lose it would feel doubtful whether to will this principle; they would be divided between the advantages of not having to give and the disadvantages of never receiving unremunerated help. (iii) and (iv), it seems to me, state the substance of (i) above.

(v) 'I propose to help no one' universalises into 'Let no one ever help anyone'. This principle would preclude even the mutual help given in bargains and would lead to a society, if it could be called such, in which there are no services, paid or unpaid, no barter or commerce, no division of labour and no love. Men would bask in their corners or pass by or over one another like reptiles in a cage.

From Kant's rather impressionistic accounts of his argument we may, therefore, draw the conclusion that the selfish maxim, according as it is stated and universalised, leads to self-contradiction, or would result in forms of society which are more or less unacceptable to thinking and feeling human beings.

VI. THE MORAL MOTIVE

We now come to a particularly difficult aspect of Kant's ethics – his account of the moral motive. So far we have seen that Kant held that the moral value of an action depends upon the intention of the individual who performs it and that an act has moral value only if it is done 'from duty'. This means that it must not merely *accord with* what duty requires, but must be done *for the sake of* fulfilling the agent's duty. An act might accord with duty if done from fear of punishment or with a view to some other personal advantage, but it would not then have moral value. This is easy to understand, and many would agree with Kant thus far. Kant also believed, however, that an act done from duty is as such done for the sake of fulfilling the pure *a priori* moral law, and this is not so easy to understand. According to Kant, a law is pure when the expression of it contains no empirical concepts. Now the moral laws prohibiting murder and theft do contain empirical concepts. The concept of murder, for example, contains the empirical notion of killing. The pure *a priori* moral law must therefore, as we have seen, be more fundamental than such specific moral principles and be expressed in the form of the Principle of Universal Law: 'Act only on that maxim through which you can at the same time will that it should become a universal law.'

This supreme principle of morality is pure, in that it does not specifically refer to actions such as murder which have to be defined, at any rate in part, in empirical terms. On the other hand, it does refer to such actions indirectly, through the notion of a maxim, since a maxim is the principle of action which an individual in fact adopts. Furthermore, the very first word of the imperative seems to involve the empirical notion of an action. In the *Groundwork* Kant himself says that the good will that is essential to moral action is not a mere wish but 'the summoning of all means so far as they are in our power'.[43] The 'means' here referred to must be the means existing in the natural world that have to be utilised in order to do such things as keep one's word or help other people. 'Act only on that maxim', therefore, entails empirical notions, and the Categorical Imperative cannot be pure in any very strict sense.

When Kant says that a principle is *a priori* he means that it is necessary and universal. He believes, therefore, that the Categorical Imperative confers an inevitability and inescapability upon moral principles like that of the truths of mathematics. It is no more possible to reject or alter a genuine moral demand than it is to refuse to believe that $3 = 1 + 2$. And just as any conceivable triple equals the sum of one and two, so it is always right to keep promises and to help those who need it. Attempts to establish the moral law by reference to the nature of men and of what happens in the world serve only to give excuses for evading the demands of morality. Even if no one ever obeyed the command of the moral law, and even if everyone were selfish and maleficent, the moral law would be valid always and for everyone.[44]

Kant does seem to give an unacceptably abstract account of the moral motive. In the *Groundwork* he says: '... since I have deprived the will of all impulses which could arise from the following of any particular law, nothing remains over that could serve the will as its principle except the universal conformity to law of its actions generally.'[45] In the *Critique of Practical Reason* Kant says that since all 'material practical principles' are determined by self-love or desire for one's own happiness, for a rational being who is to act for the sake of the moral law 'nothing remains' – the same phrase as in the *Groundwork* – except to be motivated by 'the mere form of a universal legislation'.[46] What is difficult to accept in these statements is the idea that apart from, and possibly opposed to, the natural impulses there is a pure rational will which can act merely in order to achieve universality. Even if we grant the possibility of a pure rational will, it is difficult to see how it could will to bring about a mere rational universality.

We can make better sense of Kant's words, however, if we suppose that in using the phrase 'nothing remains' he is not saying that a pure rational will could exist and act, but is intellectually abstracting the concept of moral rationality. We have already seen that Kant's very expression of the Categorical Imperative involves acting in the world and the adoption of maxims to be followed there. A man who makes promise-keeping one of his maxims of behaviour is adopting a principle of action that could be followed by everyone. Each time he keeps a promise he ignores or discards the idea of doing something that could advantage him but could not be done by everyone. Keeping promises will generally be of advantage to himself, but he would be acting from duty if he would have kept his promise even if by so doing he would have been disadvantaged. In that event, what 'determines' his action, to use a word that Kant is fond of, is his rational concern not to do what he could not recommend everyone to do. His keeping his promise is 'at the same time' – Kant's own phrase – his obedience to the principle of Universal Law. Paton expresses the argument effectively as follows: 'The attempt to stand outside our personal maxims and estimate impartially and impersonally their fitness to be principles of action for others than ourselves is the necessary condition of all moral judgment . . .'[47]

It might be suggested that if Kant is interpreted in this way his view is being watered down so as to become much more like that of Hume than Kant could have allowed. For although Hume regarded feelings or sentiments as the basis of morality, he nevertheless said that moral sentiments differ from non-moral ones in that when we make moral judgments we 'correct' our own feelings so as to bring them into line with what other people can accept or with what a 'judicious observer' would judge proper. Even though, for example, a man may be our enemy, we can bring ourselves to view him as he would appear to someone who does not feel injured by him as we do, and this is the sort of adjustment that transforms interested feelings into disinterested moral sentiments. Kant, I think, was more concerned with will and action than Hume was, but their very different philosophical outlooks do not keep them from a measure of agreement in their accounts of morality. It would, indeed, have been strange if these two great philosophers had been wholly and utterly at odds in their attempts to analyse the same thing. When Hume gives a detailed account of the difference between the moral sentiments and other feelings he says that it is by means of the imagination that we take this more general view and that it might loosely and improperly be called reason. Reason is being reinstated under another name. Reason breaks out, so to say, from Hume's 'sentiments', just as experience is uncovered when we examine Kant's 'pure *a priori* moral law'. What is common to them both is the idea that moral rules are not mere personal maxims but are impersonal and objective in the sense that they force or impose themselves on particular individuals much as the facts of nature do.

There is, however, a very important difference between the views of Hume and of Kant on the part played by reason in morality, and an examination of it will help in the further understanding of Kant's moral philosophy. Hume – apart from what we have just said about 'correcting' the feelings – only allows to reason the function of being 'the slave of the passions', of showing men how to satisfy their desires and achieve their aims. Reason, therefore, is parasitic on desires and aims, and it does not make sense to say that these are either rational or irrational. But Kant, as we have seen, considered that the reason functions *both* in the discovering of means for satisfying our desires or for achieving happiness *and* in propounding the moral law and requiring submission to it. His doctrine of the Categorical Imperative, indeed, was meant to indicate this very thing. Not only are there 'objective laws of reason' which enable hypothetical imperatives to be framed but the moral law stated in the Categorical Imperative is rational and objective too. In technical and prudential imperatives reason is subordinated to the passions, but in moral contexts it is their guide and rightful master. According to Kant, therefore, reason has a practical as well as a theoretical aspect, and can therefore guide action as well as make inferences and discover the truth.

If reason were only theoretical it would be occupied only in finding out what is true or false and in endeavouring to draw correct inferences. It would enable us to find out whether the satisfaction of one sort of desire helped or hindered the satisfaction of another, but it would not enable us to decide that one desire ought to be satisfied rather than another. If actions result from desires reason would not, then, enable us to decide which actions ought to be performed. Decisions to give scope to one sort of desire and action rather than another would be beyond the competence of reason. But according to Kant, reason does provide guidance between types of desire and action, in that it prohibits those which could not be willed by everyone and requires performance of the duties of promise-keeping, beneficence and the rest. 'Everyone ought to help others' limits the scope that is permissible in the pursuit of personal satisfactions. A man who decides not to help anyone else is not merely choosing to live a *different* life from others, as a man might opt for life in the country or life in the town, but is choosing *wrongly*, is going against what the pure practical reason demands. A man's reason does not only tell him how best to get what he most desires but also how he ought to limit his actions in so doing.

We may illustrate this by contrast to a contemporary account of human choice. In the complex societies we inhabit there is a great deal of public voluntary work that has to be undertaken if the system is to operate as a whole. This falls upon a few people who tend to be overloaded with boring or even distressing tasks. It has been pointed out that those who take on these jobs are not acting as 'rational, self-interested individuals' should if they do not obtain more than corresponding benefits (in the form, perhaps, of public honours or satisfaction of their desire for power) to offset their trouble.[48] According to this view, it is possible that society is upheld by foolish, irrational men who just do not know what is good for them and allow themselves to be exploited by others. But if Kant's account of what is rational is correct, at any rate some of these people are following the call of duty from the motive of not omitting to do something, the omission of which by everyone could not be willed by anyone. The contemporary view I have just referred to results from applying the economic principle of the rational maximisation of individual satisfactions to the whole social sphere without placing any limitation upon it. On Kantian principles this is not reasonable, since it fails to recognise that reason extends beyond the satisfactions of the individual and requires behaviour that relates to everyone.

VII. THE PRINCIPLE OF AUTONOMY AND OTHER FORMULATIONS OF THE CATEGORICAL IMPERATIVE

Near the beginning of the *Groundwork* Kant says that when a maxim is rejected because it cannot be willed to become a universal law this rejection is not made 'because of a prospective loss to you or even to others, but because it cannot fit as a principle into a possible legislation of universal law'.[49] We notice in this a reference to a system of legislation into which the rules governing men's actions must be capable of being harmoniously accommodated. The idea is given more definite expression farther on when Kant states the so-called Formula of Autonomy, according to which the individual is required so to act '*that the will through its maxim could at the same time regard itself as legislating universally*'.[50] Kant also expresses this legal aspect of his view in the so-called Kingdom of Ends formula as follows: 'Every rational being must so act as if he were through his maxim always a legislating member in the universal Kingdom of Ends.'[51] The word 'autonomy' and the phrase 'universal legislation' are used in the *Critique of Practical Reason*, but Kant does not there distinguish different formulations of the Categorical Imperative. Indeed, he there states the 'Fundamental Law of the Pure Practical Reason' in the form: 'Act so that the maxim of your will can always at the same time hold good as a principle of universal legislation.'[52] Here, it will be seen, the notion of legislation, which is akin to but not the same as that of law, is brought right into the basic formulation of the Categorical Imperative. In the *Groundwork*, but not in the *Critique of Practical Reason*, another formulation is introduced between the Universal Law formula and the Autonomy formula. This is: '*So act that you treat humanity in your own person and in the person of everyone else always at the same time as an end and never merely as means.*'[53]

It will be convenient if we start with some discussion of this last formula. The introduction of the notion of an end is surprising, if we remember that in his account of the good will Kant had said that it is not good on account of the end it seeks. Furthermore, in the Universal Law formula empirical notions are not directly or obviously present – unless we regard the imperative verb 'act' as obviously empirical – whereas here the empirical concept 'humanity' is directly referred to. Professor Singer is not much impressed by this formula as Kant expresses it, and says that it 'has more of an emotional uplift than a definite meaning'.[54] It has also been pointed out that when Kant was writing the *Groundwork*, a book he had been promising to write for many years past, he had very much on his mind a commentary on Cicero's *de Finibus* published by his friend Christian Garve in 1783, and was trying to deal with it in a friendly yet critical way. According to Cicero, a man who sees no harm in injuring others abolishes what is human in man (*omnino hominem ex homine tollit*), whereas the interests of all men should be the concern of all.[55] It is quite possible that Kant was weaving this idea into his exposition in order to show that his account of the Categorical Imperative could make room for one of the Stoic principles which Cicero and Garve had thought important. How, then, is the Principle of the End in Itself, or the Principle of Personality, as Singer calls it, related to the Principle of Universal Law, and does the former add anything to what the latter says?

Kant's own answer is not easy to follow, but his most convincing point seems to be this. The Principle of Universal Law limits the actions of each individual to those which all men could do or will. In choosing his maxims, therefore, each individual ought to have a concern for the scope of choice of everyone else. No individual, therefore, can be left out from the range of those for which each ought to have a concern.[56] Kant also distinguishes between things and persons. Things have relative value only and are sought only for the satisfaction or happiness they can bring. Persons, on the other hand, have absolute value and exist as ends in themselves. Persons, therefore, are objective ends which ought to be the concern of all rational beings, whereas things can only be subjective ends which depend upon contingent and changeable desires. When, therefore, persons are said to be ends in themselves it is also being said that everyone ought to recognise and respect everyone.[57]

As Kant shows, the wrongness of treating human beings as means only is illustrated by the case of lying promises. Deceit and fraud are the manipulation of one person for the sole benefit of the other. Kant does not say so, but no doubt he had it very much in mind that slavery and other forms of exploitation also consist in treating persons as if they existed only for the benefit of their exploiters and not as ends in themselves. But a malevolent individual can humiliate without cheating or exploiting. Indeed, his insults are all the more effective if the person who is insulted is more than a mere means to malicious pleasure. Again, envy is often the vice of the exploited, and need not involve cheating or exploitation. Kant's use of 'merely' echoes Cicero's use of *omnino* and shows he was aware of the fact that we must make use of one another in some ways, as when we buy and sell or ask favours. We are not, then, to use persons as means only, but only to some extent. Kant does not say what we have to do if we are to treat one another as ends as well as means, not does he give any help as to how much we can use one another. An advantage of the Principle of Universal Law, therefore, is that it gives more specific instructions about how maxims of conduct are to be shown to be morally unacceptable. It is, moreover, more comprehensive, in that it can be applied to types of wrongdoing which escape the net cast by the Principle of Personality.

Let us now consider the Principle of Autonomy, an examination of which reveals what is most important and characteristic in Kant's ethics. The formulation given on p. 35 above is a literal translation of the German text. Abbott translates Kant's words as follows: '[act so that] *the will could at the same time regard itself as giving in its maxims universal laws*'. Paton's version runs: '[act so that] *the will can regard itself as at the same time making universal law by means of its maxim*'. It will be seen that I used the word 'legislating', Abbot wrote 'giving . . . universal laws' and Paton 'making universal law'. An examination of these differences will help us to understand what Kant intended to say. Common to all three translations, of course, is the idea of legislation. Kant is saying that no rule of action is morally acceptable that cannot be regarded as a law applicable *to* everyone – this is the emphasis of the Universal Law formula – and legislated *by* everyone – this is the emphasis in the Principle of Autonomy and in the Kingdom of Ends formula. Each individual is to regard 'the will' as legislating for everyone, including himself. I translated Kant's word *gesetzgebend* literally, Abbott still more literally, in terms of the German roots for law and for giving, while Paton writes of *making* laws. The reason that Paton gives for not accepting Abbott's translation is that it is important to make it clear that 'the word "universal" qualifies the law, not the making'. This, I suggest, is not relevant, since it is the use of 'make' for 'give' which is important.

Minutiae of translation can appear tiresome, but it is very important that we get them right on this occasion. 'Making', it seems to me, imports a notion of production or manufacture that is foreign to Kant's intention. It also carries an implication of beginning to exist which is also at variance with Kant's view of the moral law. At one place in the *Groundwork*, it is true, Kant does say that *the will* can regard itself as author of the law. But in two important passages elsewhere he makes a point of denying that the giver of the moral law, its legislator, can be its author. One of these passages occurs in the *Lectures on Ethics*, which were delivered 1780–2, not long before he wrote the *Groundwork*, and the other in the *Metaphysic of Morals*, which was published in 1797. In the *Lectures on Ethics* he says that 'no being, not even the divine being, is an author of moral laws, since they do not originate from choice but are practically necessary. If they were not necessary it could also be that lying would be a virtue'.[58] In the *Metaphysic of Morals* Kant writes that a legislator can only be the author of contingent, positive or arbitrary laws, In this same passage Kant says that 'the law which binds us *a priori* and unconditionally by means of our own reason can also be expressed as proceeding from the will of a supreme lawgiver, i.e. of one who has only rights and no duties (accordingly, from the Divine Will). But this only signifies the Idea of a moral being whose will is law for all, without his being conceived as the author of the law.'[59] We can take it that these two passages indicate Kant's settled view. The moral law just is not the sort of thing which, like positive law, can be decided according to the choice of a legislator. Not even God could so make it, any more than God could be author of the fact that a triangle has three angles. (This example is given by Kant in the *Lectures on Ethics*.) When, as in Judaism and Christianity, the moral law is regarded as proceeding from the will of God, this can only mean that we can rationally construct the concept of a being who only wills what is right for all rational beings to do. What cannot be made or chosen by God, cannot be made or chosen by men. Kant would have been astonished and alarmed at the Existentialist idea that a man can and should make his own morality.

Nevertheless, although the moral law cannot be arbitrarily made either by God or men, it obliges us through 'our own reason' or rational will. From one point of view, it would be absurd to say that we each have 'our *own* reason', for it is our desires and personal tastes that are peculiarly our own, and reason is not personal, but universal. This, indeed, is the essential teaching of the Principle of Universal Law. But on the other hand, it could hardly be said that an individual is acting rationally if he merely follows a command that has been made to him. People can be trained to obey orders which they cannot see any point in. An individual might understand a command that nevertheless appears quite pointless, as would be the case, for example, if he were ordered to throw some precious object in the sea. A man so instructed might think that his commander did not know that the object was valuable. But if the commander, after having been told of its value, still insisted that it must be thrown away the man under orders would still want to know what other reason there could be for destroying it. If there were none the command would be arbitrary and irrational. If it turned out that the commander merely wanted to assert himself, then the command would be hypothetically rational in the sense that it was a means of satisfying the commander's desire for self-assertion. But the man being commanded would be behaving merely as a means to this if he saw no point in the exercise of this self-assertion. If he thought it a good thing that his commander's sense of importance should be flattered, then in obeying he would not be merely a means but also supporting something he himself approved of. This sort of thing could happen in various groups the members of which were all agreed on its purposes. Within a group, therefore, commands are rational when any member, on reflection, would recognise that following it would promote the interests of the group. But morality, according to Kant, is not concerned with the interests of a limited group, but with the possibility of a universal community of free men. In such a community no one would be required to do anything which he would not think it reasonable for everyone to do. It would not matter to him whether he was receiving or giving the command. In obeying it he would be doing what he thought reasonable. It would be as if he himself had given the order.

The nature of this idea can be made plainer if we contrast such free obedience with forced obedience. When disobedience to a law brings a penalty with it the man who obeys may do so in order to avoid the penalty. In this case his motive is his own safety or comfort, and hence his action, though legal, is not morally good, since it accords with duty but is not done for the sake of duty. Obedience to the moral law, therefore, is obedience for the sake of the law, and as it is not the result of fear, is freely given. Hence, Kant says that moral laws are 'laws of freedom'.[60] To obey God's commands from fear of Hell or for rewards in Heaven is not to act morally at all. Those who act from duty are doing what they regard as reasonable. What is reasonable is not merely what furthers the individual's own interests but what would bring his actions into harmony with those of other men in so far as they are reasonable too. In acting for the sake of the moral law men are controlling their desires and regulating their interests so that they can live together under a law that they all recognise. We have seen that Kant distinguished action from inclination or the desire for happiness from wholly rational action. This last he attributed to the will. In so far as the will determines a man's action, he is not concerned only with himself, but with the limitation of his interests by those of all other reasonable men in a community which they all both promote and conform to. The will or 'our own reason' is not personal, but is, to speak metaphorically, an inlet through which the general will of humanity can enter and enable the individual to control his personal needs and desires.

It should not be supposed that this means that the supreme end of man is the promotion of the material happiness of all. For one thing, Kant believed that there are many other duties besides that of promoting the happiness of others. For another, if the happiness of mankind were the supreme end of man, duty and the moral law would be subordinated to it and man would have surrendered his rational autonomy. The moral law is not a means of providing for everyone the pleasures that each would like for himself – this, in the words of the nineteenth-century neo-Kantian philosopher Hermann Cohen, would be like establishing a mere 'comradeship of worms' in which all their movements were smoothly integrated. Such an integration could be made possible only after extensive scientific research, and would require thereafter frequent departures from the rules thereby established, in order to maximise happiness in unexpected circumstances. This would mean that there would have to be scientific experts about how men ought to live, and those without this knowledge would have to act on the advice or under the orders of those who have it. According to Kant, 'there is no need of science or philosophy for knowing what a man has to do in order to be honest and good',[61] and to rest morality on empirical matters is to endanger its very existence. To make it a matter for research and expertise would destroy the autonomy that is the basis of its universality. 'Scientific' morality would be an even greater hindrance to human freedom than the morality of divine commands has been in the past.

According to the Principle of Humanity, the dignity of each individual man is an essential requirement of the moral law, and according to the Principle of Autonomy, the moral law is both actively willed by every rational being and regarded by him as the law he should submit to. These principles have a liberal, even a democratic air, and Kant's other notion of a universal Kingdom of Ends in which all men are legislating members extends the ethical into a somewhat political sphere. The views expressed in the *Groundwork* concentrated in a closely reasoned form much that was being said by other writers of the time. In his *Dialogues Philosophiques* in 1768 Voltaire had written:

B. What do you call just and unjust?
A. What seems so to the universe as a whole.

Apart from such adumbrations of the Universal Law formula, we may also notice appeals to the Principle of Humanity. In 1779 *Nathan der Weise* was published, the the play in which Lessing showed the moral irrelevance of sectarian and national differences.

> Was heisst denn Volk?
> Sind Christ und Jude eher Christ und Jude
> Als Mensch?

In 1784, when Kant was writing the *Groundwork*, the *Barber of Seville* appeared in Paris, and was immediately regarded as an attack on aristocratic distinctions of rank. Beaumarchais, its author, had earlier been active in persuading Louis XVI to bring France into alliance with the American colonists in their war with the British Crown. In that same year Kant himself wrote in an article entitled *What is Enlightenment?* 'The touchstone of everything that can be concluded as a law for a people lies in the question whether the people could have imposed such a law upon itself.'[62] According to Kant, enlightenment is 'the escape of men from their self-incurred tutelage', and his principles of Humanity, Autonomy and the Kingdom of Ends may be regarded as connecting the emancipatory movement of his times with what is permanent in the moral law.

But the greatest contemporary influence on the way in which Kant stated his ethical theory was Rousseau. Kant read Rousseau's writings, sometimes with approval, often with irritation, but always with admiration for his splendid style. In some notes written about 1764–5 Kant says that at one time he had despised the ignorant masses, and that Rousseau taught him to honour men and so to be able to give worth to others and to establish the rights of humanity. In his *Dreams of a Spirit-Seer* written about the same time Kant mentions the possibility of a '*felt dependence* of the private will upon the general will'.[63] The General Will, of course, is the central notion of Rousseau's *Social Contract* (1762). There are some close similarities between what Rousseau says, without much argument, in Book I of that celebrated book, and the views which Kant worked out and analysed in the *Groundwork*. In Book I, chapter VIII of the *Social Contract* Rousseau says that in the passage from the state of nature to the civil state justice replaces instinct, 'the voice of duty' replaces 'physical impulse', and that man, who had hitherto consulted his own interest, now has to 'consult his reason rather than study his inclinations'. Furthermore, when civil society has been formed, man is no longer a slave to his appetites, but acquires 'moral freedom', and this involves 'obedience to a law one prescribes to oneself'. It is also interesting to note Book I, chapter VI, in which Rousseau says that when a body politic has been formed all its members constitute *a people*, and they are *citizens* in so far as they are legislators, and *subjects* in so far as they put themselves under the laws of the state.

Kant was not concerned with the state or with political philosophy in the *Groundwork*, but his moral theory there is presented in a form which has implications for law and politics. We may put Kant's argument in the following way. As his examples show, he wanted to know how things would be if people universally adopted maxims that go against the fundamental principles of morality. The principle of Universal Law was intended to show that *some* people could go against them but would then be parasitic on the trust of the others, but that if *all* were to do so, basic practices or society itself would be rendered impossible. According to the Principle of Humanity, going against the laws of morality would involve treating people as things to be used rather than as persons to be respected. Finally, maxims that transgress the moral law would lead men into subjection to rules which could not be recognised as just by everyone. These negations presuppose a positive ideal, that of a community, every member in which is respected by all the others, and in which only those rules of conduct are followed which everyone recognises to be reasonable. This, Kant believed, is the Idea of Reason implicit in the moral principles which civilised peoples of all creeds and nations recognise. In the *Critique of Pure Reason* Kant had said that legislation – and he was here thinking of the laws of states – ought to be guided by the Idea – and in using this word he had Plato in mind – of 'a constitution *of the greatest human freedom, according to laws which enable the freedom of each to exist along with the freedom of others* (without any regard to the greatest human happiness, because that must necessarily follow by itself) . . .'[64] What had appeared in the *Critique of Pure Reason* as a political ideal, appears in the *Groundwork* as the ideal presupposed in the principles of morality, and is seen to be the supreme principle of morality, the Moral Law itself.

VIII. FREEDOM OF THE WILL AND MORALITY

Whether the will is free or whether everything is subject to natural necessity is one of the main questions which Kant tried to settle in the *Critique of Pure Reason*. The answer he there gave to the question is that when the actions and choices of men are regarded as events in the spatio-temporal world they must be subject to empirical laws, and hence they cannot be free but must be determined. If we adopt the position of theoretical *observers* trying to *explain* men's actions, then inevitably we regard some act, say, of malicious lying as the act of a man whose heredity, education and environment made it certain that he would act in this way. If we had complete knowledge of his origins and circumstances we should be able to predict exactly what he would do. But in spite of all this, Kant observes, we impute this man's offence to him and blame him for it. When we do this we are no longer explaining his action as a psychologist might, but are considering it in the light of *practical* reason. As a natural event his act was inevitable, but nevertheless he ought not to have done it. If he ought not to have told this lie but nevertheless did, it must have been possible for him to have refrained from telling it, and since all the natural impulses and desires and circumstances brought it about, some non-natural motive must have been available to him to enable him to desist from the lie. 'Another causality, that of freedom', called by Kant 'transcendental freedom', must have been able to alter his conduct, even though in fact it did not. But if this is so, Kant continues, it follows that we regard this act of lying as completely undetermined by relation to the man's previous condition, 'as if the offender started off a series of effects completely by himself'. He goes on:

This blame is founded on a law of reason by which we regard the reason as a cause which, independently of all the above-mentioned empirical conditions, could and should have determined the man's actions in another way. We do not indeed regard the causality of reason as something that merely accompanies the action, but as something complete in itself, even if the sensible motives do not favour but even oppose the action; the action is imputed to the man's intelligible character and he is wholly guilty now, in the very moment when he lies; therefore the reason was wholly free, notwithstanding all the empirical conditions of the act, and the deed has to be wholly imputed to this failure of reason.[65]

This is a remarkable thesis. Kant considers that everything a man does is in principle subject to scientific explanation in terms of natural causes, and is hence determined. This is how the man appears to an observer. But in spite of this the man is held responsible for his actions, and this can only mean that he could have acted differently, and this, in its turn, means that reason, 'another causality', could have initiated a different series of actions without itself being an effect of any previous cause. The word 'previous', indeed, would be out of place in this context, since this 'other causality' can initiate actions but cannot be located in any spatio-temporal causal series. Kant even distinguishes between an empirical and an intelligible character. The former is in time and is subject to scientific explanation and capable of being the basis for predictions of what a man will do. The latter is not in time, and is therefore not subject to scientific explanation, but is the aspect of a man which makes him liable to moral praise or condemnation. The practical attitude involved in the imputation of responsibility presupposes that the will is free to initiate actions which, when looked at from a purely theoretical point of view, can be fully explained as effects of causes, and might, furthermore, be predicted with certainty.

Another argument of somewhat similar form is given in the *Critique of Practical Reason*. Kant there asks his readers to consider whether a man's actions must always be determined by his desires. He imagines a man who is threatened with immediate death on a gallows erected outside his house should he give way to an appetite which he says is irresistible. This man's desire to live would lead him to refrain from giving way to this appetite and would prove that it was not irresistible. But suppose, Kant continues, that the king commands this man, again with the threat of immediate execution, to bear false witness against someone the king wishes to destroy. The threatened man might not feel sure that he would in these circumstances overcome his desire to live, 'But he must unhesitatingly admit that it is possible for him. He judges, therefore, that he can do a thing because he is conscious that he ought to do it, and he recognises in himself the freedom which, but for the moral law, would have remained unknown to him.'[66]

Common to these two arguments is the claim that freedom of the will is presupposed by our moral beliefs. According to the first argument, the imputation of moral responsibility would not be justified if the individual were not free to choose between acting rightly or wrongly. According to the second argument, it could not be anyone's moral duty to act against contrary desires unless he were free to do so. Freedom to override the natural desires is a presupposition of morality. Hence the deterministic implications of the theoretical reason do not exclude the libertarian presuppositions of the practical reason. Freedom of the will is not something that could be observed by introspection. Nor could it be proved by theoretical arguments, whether these be *a priori* or empirical, that is, the freedom of the will cannot be proved by metaphysics or established by the methods of the natural sciences or of psychology. But it is a presupposition of the moral law, which is recognised by all as practically necessary.

There is a good deal of force in Kant's argument that our conception of human nature should not be formed exclusively in terms of the theoretical understanding. But does it follow that there is 'another causality', that of the *a priori* practical reason, that can determine our actions? Might it not be that the theoretical understanding acts in support of our desires, whether for our own satisfaction or for the happiness of mankind? We have seen, however, that Kant would regard this as the subjection of rational man to irrational external forces, as the abandonment of autonomy for heteronomy. According to Kant, the practical reason makes it possible for men to try to impose on things as they are an order through which they may come closer to how they ought to be.

This they can do under the guidance of the purely rational Ideal of a community in which everyone is respected and no one is forced to obey a law he does not recognise to be just. It is this Ideal that regulates the actions of those who try to do their duty. They are not determined to action by self-interest, nor by sympathy, which is limited and irregular, but by the purely rational Idea of a Kingdom of Ends. A purely rational spontaneity from an intelligible world we can conceive but not experience alters the course of events in the natural world. This intelligible world, as we have seen, is inhabited by intelligible characters, of which the empirical characters in the natural world are temporal and temporary manifestations.

It is possible to allow that there is force in the argument from moral responsibility and moral obligation to freedom of the will without concluding, as Kant does, that rational freedom must have its base, so to say, in a supra-natural noumenal world. In this connection it is useful to compare with those of Kant the views of Thomas Reid, Adam Smith's successor in the chair of moral philosophy at Glasgow. In his *Essays on the Active Powers of Man*, published in 1788, the same year as Kant's *Critique of Practical Reason*, Reid argued, like Kant, that if we have moral duties – and we do –it must be possible for us to fulfil them. He argued, too, that if the will were not free, either there would be no use for such terms as accountability, praise and blame, merit and demerit, or they would have to be given new meanings. But he does not conclude from this that there is a phenomenal will that is subject to the necessity of nature and a noumenal will that somehow affects the natural will from the intelligible world. It is Kant's conception of nature that leads him to argue in this way. 'Psychological causality', he writes, subjects man to natural necessity as much as 'mechanical causality' does.[67] Kant believed he had proved in the *Critique of Pure Reason* that everything that happens in the natural world is subject to causal necessity, and that unless this were so experience of an objective world would be impossible. Reid, who was not encumbered by the doctrines of the *Critique of Pure Reason*, thought that if freedom of the will is to be established, animal motives should be distinguished from rational motives.

48

As in mechanics motion is proportional to the force, so in animal life the strongest motive always prevails. This is one reason why we do not regard animals as accountable for their actions and do not blame them. But rational motives 'do not give a blind impulse to the will' as animal motives do; 'they convince but . . . do not impel'. Men are in the natural world, but their rational motives are less like mechanical movements than are the impulses of animals. We may speak of the mechanism of matter, and even of the quasi-mechanism of animals, but human motives have to be looked at in very different terms. If we wished to state Reid's position in Kantian language we could say that according to Reid the category of rational motivation is essential if we are to make sense of human behaviour.[67a] It would follow that attempts to understand and predict human actions by means of causal laws are bound to be unsatisfactory. Incidentally, Reid pointed out that rational motives are not existences or events located in time, and therefore it does not make sense to say that they can be in causal relationships with other events.[68] This may well be a more adequate expression of the point that Kant was making when he wrote of non-temporal intelligible characters.

A further difficulty in Kant's view of the *nature* of freedom of the will, as distinct from his argument that morality presupposes its *existence* and *operation*, is that the contrast between the natural and the intelligible world seems to leave no place for human history as an empirical study. Those deeds of men which historians describe are established as the result of empirical enquiry, and although from time to time enthusiasts like Condorcet have said that successful predictions of the human future are bound to come, they have not come yet. In the *Critique of Practical Reason* Kant says that if we could get sufficient insight into human motives human actions would be as predictable as eclipses, and so he seems to be on the side of Condorcet. In his *Idea for a Universal History from a Cosmopolitan Standpoint* (1784) Kant writes of human actions as 'appearances' of free will, and says that although individual choices influence particular events, human history as a whole is subject to laws 'as stable as the unstable weather'.[69]

49

Meteorology, even today, allows fewer exact predictions than astronomy does, but it is a natural science that takes no account of human purposes except in so far as men can make use of its predictions. Furthermore, in this article Kant considers the possibility that Nature has purposes which the men who work and struggle are not aware of. The rational motives of individuals are thus depreciated and made subordinate to a plan which men have not themselves devised. It is true that Kant calls this 'philosophical history', which he distinguishes from the work of 'practicing empirical historians', but it is not clear what view he takes of the latter. If it is not to be treated in causal terms, and if the deeds of men who try to fulfil the moral law are to play any part in it whatsoever, it must be removed from the sphere of causal necessity and at the same time possess spatial and temporal properties which cannot be attributed to the merely intelligible or noumenal world. There is no place for such an enquiry in Kant's philosophical scheme.

Kant's position, then, is that in the empirical world, the world of appearances, determinism is complete, while in the intelligible world, the world of noumena, freedom of the will is possible and must be presupposed by those who accept the validity of the moral law. The intelligible world is not the world of time and space, and Kant seems to have thought that there is a timeless element in morality. I find his discussion of the matter interesting, though obscure, and I shall therefore mention a few of the points he raises.

On pp. 45-6 above a passage was quoted from the *Critique of Pure Reason* in which Kant says that when a man commits a wrong action it is imputed to his intelligible character and he is wholly guilty in the moment when he commits it. Kant seems to be arguing that if someone does wrong nothing that went before can alter his guilt. He may have had a bad start in life, and he may have had bad luck subsequently, but this does not affect the evil of his deed, which is his evil, introduced into the world by him. As a free agent, he it was who initiated the evil. A wrong, then, does not cease to be a wrong on account of what went before it. Nor, according to Kant, can its evil be expunged by what comes afterwards. A man feels remorse when he reflects on an evil he has done, and although he may try to pretend that it was a mistake or an accident, he knows quite well that if it were he would feel regret but not remorse. But what is the point of remorse, it will be said, if the evil deed, once done, cannot be undone? Kant argues, however, that remorse is not a hopeless attempt to undo what we have done, but the painful recognition that we freely did what was wrong. The guilt of the wrongdoer can no more be altered by what came after his act than by what went before it, and the guilt remains the same however long the period that has elapsed. Kant remarks that when it is a matter of 'the law of our intelligible existence (the moral law)' the reason 'recognises no distinction of time'.[70] Someone might make reparation, when this is possible, and he might amend his life, but this cannot retrospectively annul what he did when he did wrong.

Whether these considerations give support to Kant's account of the intelligible character may, however, still be doubted. For although a man's guilt cannot be altered by what went before or after, his wrong acts are committed in the natural world, and the irrelevance of time to them is due to two facts. As regards past misfortunes, their irrelevance is that if the wrongdoer is free and could have refrained from doing the wrong he cannot be excused. As regards the subsequent lapse of time, this cannot alter the guilt incurred by the deed, whatever the wrongdoer's subsequent conduct may have been, just as – indeed, just because – true statements relating to a particular point of time cannot be rendered untrue by what is done afterwards. This, if true, is very important. For it makes guilt a matter of fact and truth, unalterable by subsequent changes in the wishes, hopes and sentiments of the wrongdoer himself or of other people. Sentiments can change, and even Hume's 'judicious spectator' is imagined, and imaginations can be altered, but the practical reason is held by Kant to judge in terms that are 'not arbitrary and cannot be avoided'. Historians may apply blacking or whitewash, but the moral quality of the deeds they relate is in no way affected.

According to Kant, a man who tries to excuse a wrong act by reference to his heredity and circumstances is, so to say, rationally abandoning his rationality. Rationality is spontaneous and un-caused, and to *argue* that one could not help it is to say that one is a passive subject of external stimuli in the very breath in which one shows that one is not. Rationality is essentially free and auto-nomous, and the possessor of it necessarily regards himself as free. But Kant did not believe he had provided a metaphysical proof of the freedom of the will. If we recognise the obligations which morality places upon us we *ipso facto* regard ourselves as free, for we accept the moral law as consonant with our practical reason, and we presuppose our ability to conform to it. As long as freedom is, from a theoretical point of view, a possibility, there is no need for us to worry if no theoretical proof of it has been provided. From a practical point of view a free will must be attri-buted to all rational beings.[71]

Kant here presents a new and distinctive type of argument. Freedom of the will is not proved theoretically, but is, to use Kant's own word, 'presupposed' in our acceptance of the moral law. In deciding whether the will is free, in deciding what would seem to be a matter of fact, weight is given to the fact that we recognise we have duties and thereby assume that we are free to fulfil them. We are justified in accepting what is presupposed in the rational moral demands which we both accept and place upon ourselves. Morality somehow licences us to suppose that things are true which conflict with the views we must take of the natural world. We shall examine further aspects of this view in the next chapter.

IX. GOD AND IMMORTALITY

From what has been said so far it is clear that Kant rejected the idea that God has *made* the moral law and has imposed it on men with the threat of punishment if they do not obey it. If men obeyed the moral law because of this they would be acting prudentially, in order to avoid the pains of Hell and to obtain the pleasures of Heaven. Furthermore, according to Kant's Principle of Autonomy, in obeying the moral law an individual obeys a law which he recognises as his. Morality, as Kant understands it, requires the individual who is subject to it to be citizen and sovereign as well as subject. The moral law links rational beings together in a community that transcends nature because the Idea of it can be the motive which freely controls the natural desires of each member. This view could be described as non-theological, in that according to it morality can be analysed and, apparently, pursued, without any necessary reference to divine commands. It could also be described as anti-theological, in that it is incompatible with the sort of utilitarian or prudential theology that was widespread in the eighteenth century, according to which a man with a prudent regard for his own long-term interests would do well to obey God's orders. Yet in spite of this Kant thought it important for morality that there should be belief in God and the immortality of the soul. Of course, he did not think that these things could be proved by theoretical arguments – this was one of the central theses of the *Critique of Pure Reason*. Nor did he think that the analysis of morality showed that moral laws must be commands of God – this was dismissed by Kant as 'theological morality' or 'theological ethics'. What he did believe was that 'a conviction of the existence of a supreme being' can be 'based on moral laws'.[72] The argument appears to be of the same type as the argument for freedom of the will: the moral law is taken as categorical and apodeictic, and its necessary presuppositions are elicited.

Before proceeding further we must briefly consider Kant's doctrine of Ideas. It will have been noticed that on several occasions in earlier chapters the word 'Idea' has been printed with an initial capital letter. Kant's 'Idea' for a universal history has been referred to, as well as the 'Idea of a Kingdom of Ends', 'the Idea of a constitution of the greatest human freedom', and 'the Idea of a moral being whose will is law for all, without his being conceived as the author of the law'. We could also have quoted the phrase 'the Idea of freedom'. The capital letter is used by translaters to indicate that Kant is using his technical term '*Idee*', not the word '*Vorstellung*', which is often best translated by 'idea'.

Kant himself tells us that he was influenced by Plato's theory of forms in deciding to use the word 'Idea'. It is significant that when explaining the word in the *Critique of Pure Reason* Kant refers to Plato's *Republic* and says that a constitution with the greatest possible freedom under equal laws is 'a necessary Idea, on which not only the first plan of a constitution of the state, but all laws must be based'.[73] He then goes on to discuss certain Ideas of Reason with which metaphysics is particularly concerned. These are God, freedom and the immortality of the soul. Kant argued that no theoretical proofs could be provided to demonstrate that God exists, that the will is free and that the soul is immortal, but that these things could not be proved impossible either. Furthermore, we cannot obtain empirical knowledge of God, freedom and immortality, since they transcend anything the senses could reveal. But the Idea of a creator who has so ordered the world that a single interconnected series of purposes is at work in it has served as an impetus for the advance of knowledge and a unified conception of the world. Although we cannot know that there is any object corresponding to it, the Idea of God helps to regulate our search for knowledge. In so far as Ideas serve this function, Kant calls them 'heuristic, not ostensive concepts'[74] and even 'heuristic fictions'.[75] On the other hand, he maintained that Ideas are not arbitrarily invented, as many fictions are. We need them in order to regulate our researches, and hence they are 'necessary concepts of Reason'.[76] Kant extends his use of the word 'Idea' from these three Ideas of Reason to other sorts of ideal notion. He speaks of happiness as an Ideal of the imagination, because it takes the notion of satisfaction and develops it so as to cover the maximum satisfaction of all desires throughout a lifetime.[77] In this more extended sense Ideas are rather like Max Weber's conception of Ideal Types. For example, there are always hindrances of one sort or another to economic competition as it exists in the world, and economists have made use of the conception of 'perfect competition' as a pattern with which they can compare a given competitive market.

In the last chapter we discussed the Idea of freedom, and saw that it is established practically on the basis of the moral law. I have moral duties, and therefore I must be free to carry them out. But Kant also thought that, given the freedom presupposed in the moral law, we can go on to establish, again from a practical standpoint, the immortality of the soul and the existence of God. Morality, that is the demands of *practical* reason, forms the basis, and upon this a *practical belief* in God and immortality can be established. The arguments are set out in the *Critique of Practical Reason*, where God, Freedom and Immortality are called Postulates of Pure Practical Reason.

Now we have seen that according to Kant the only thing that is good without qualification is action done from duty, that is, moral goodness or virtue. But although, in a sense, this is the supreme good, it is not the *complete good*. People may act from duty, and hence may manifest moral goodness, in a world where wickedness and injustice prevail, and it is the duty of those who live in such a world, as we do, to endeavour to realise in it the perfect good, called by Kant the *bonum consummatum* or Supreme Good. From the point of view of an individual this means that he will bring his will into perfect accord with the demands of the moral law. He could only succeed in this by eliminating any tendency to go against the moral law and by thus achieving what Kant called a holy will. It is not possible, however, for beings who are subject to the temptations that assail them in the natural world to fulfil this duty at a given moment of time. They can only achieve this step by step in a process going on *in infinitum*, and this endless progress is only possible if the soul is immortal.

From the standpoint of the whole, the Supreme Good requires that happiness should be proportioned to virtue in such a way that those who deserve happiness and only those should have it. This is what 'impartial reason' requires, and hence it also requires 'the existence of a cause adequate to this effect', viz. the existence of God.[78] In the *Critique of Judgment* (1790) Kant gives a sombre account of a righteous man who believes neither in God nor in immortality. This man will see deceit and wickedness prevailing, and men who deserve happiness subjected to want, disease and untimely death. 'So it will be until the wide grave engulfs them all together – honest or not it makes no difference – and throws them back, these men who were able to believe themselves the final purpose of creation, into the abyss of the purposeless chaos of matter from which they were drawn.'[79] Such an atheist, Kant thinks, must either 'assume the existence of a moral author of the world' or else give up the pursuit of virtue as impossible.

This 'moral theology', or 'ethico-theology' as Kant called it, has been very severely criticised. The poet Heinrich Heine said ironically that Kant put forward his ethico-theology in order that his servant, Lampe, should not lose his faith and his happiness, or perhaps in order to keep in with the police. According to Heine, Kant is like a man who breaks all the lamps in a street, plunging it into complete darkness, and then says that he merely did it to show that it is impossible to see without them.[80] Schopenhauer, in the book referred to in section v above, said that, having argued successfully in favour of moral autonomy and against the view that morality is the prudent pursuit of happiness, Kant made a despicable about turn and went back to the theological ethics he had repudiated. Professor Walsh argues that if God is to help in apportioning happiness to virtue he must force men to co-operate – and this would destroy the moral autonomy of individuals – or else so contrive things that selfish behaviour would lead to the Supreme Good – and this would hardly encourage people to persist in virtue, since they would be bound to feel that 'God will make everything right in the end'.[81]

Heine's observations are not of much philosophical importance. Kant, no doubt, was sensitive to Lampe's feelings, but regarded as idolatry any idea that 'we can please the Supreme Being by other means than a moral disposition'.[82] To hold beliefs because they are pleasing to the public authorities would be to abandon the autonomy that is essential to morality. And although Kant claimed in the *Critique of Pure Reason* to have destroyed the theoretical *arguments* for the existence of God and for immortality, he did not claim to have abolished the corresponding *beliefs*. On the contrary, he thought he had strengthened them by separating them from metaphysical illusions. His view was that these beliefs are bound up with our acceptance of the moral law.

Schopenhauer's criticism fails too, but raises a problem which needs further discussion. Kant, as we have seen, rejects 'theological morality', that is, he rejects the view that morality is a prudential conformity to God's commands. But the practical beliefs in God and immortality are needed in order to encourage moral effort, or at any rate to lessen the discouragement that a universe known to be replete with wickedness and believed to be godless would inevitably give rise to. Practical acceptance of God and immortality is supposed by Kant to be based on 'the judgment of a disinterested reason'[83] and is not the result of baits or bribes. A man becomes a practical theist, as we may call him, not in order to gain immortality and bliss for himself but through concern for the fullest possible development of virtuous dispositions and for the establishment of justice in a world where there is too little of it. No doubt he himself would benefit if this were the outcome, but his aim is for the happiness of all, and not for happiness in itself but for happiness as deserved or merited. The problem raised by Kant's arguments is that a vivid practical belief in God and immortality could easily degenerate into the old prudential theology. Would it be possible to preserve the purity of the moral motive if the practical belief in Providence were very strong? In order to answer this we have to make a comparison between the hopelessness of the sort of moral atheism that Kant describes, a hopelessness that has become more common since his day, and the possibility that practical theism will revert to theological morality.

There is not the space to discuss Professor Walsh's objections in detail. But it is worth pointing out that Kant stresses the moral apprenticeship that would be made possible if the soul were immortal, as well as the practical significance of belief in Providence. Kant's ethico-theology is accompanied by what we may call his ethico-pneumatology, and this last allows more room for the free moral activity of rational persons and lessens, without perhaps removing altogether the need for forcible interventions by the deity.

The Kantian scholar Hans Vaihinger in his *The Philosophy of As–If* gives an eccentric but interesting account of Kant's theory about the Postulates of Pure Practical Reason. According to Vaihinger, the Transcendental Ideas are intended by Kant to be nothing but 'heuristic fictions', and this can only mean that, necessary as they are, they must not be regarded as informing us of the world as it is, but must be accepted as fictional aids both to theoretical enquiry and to rational living. Thus morality requires us to act *as if* the will were free, even though we cannot know that it is and have scientific reasons for supposing that it is not. Vaihinger thinks that his view of the Ideas gets most support in the third section of the *Groundwork*, where Kant uses such words as 'presuppose' and 'assume', and says that if we cannot act 'except *under the Idea of freedom*', it is 'as if' our will had been shown to be free by theoretical arguments. Vaihinger thinks that in the *Critique of Practical Reason* there is a tendency to move from this properly 'critical' point of view to a 'dogmatic' position in which the Ideas are taken to refer to facts in the world. Nevertheless, Kant again gave expression to the 'critical' view of the Ideas in the *Critique of Judgment* when he writes of a man whose self-reproach speaks to him 'as if it were the voice of a judge to whom he is accountable'.[84]

But Kant is almost always careful to use language that does not commit him to a 'dogmatic' view of God and immortality. He holds that we cannot know that God exists or that the soul is immortal as we know facts about the natural world. We can never link God and immortal souls as causally interacting substances in the empirical world which we inhabit along with tigers and microorganisms. These Ideas are essentially supra-natural and as such problematic. On the other hand, if men try to do what is right despite the personal losses this may bring to them, they are regulating their actions by a rule which unites them with all other persons in a free community. If hope for constant moral advance and for the establishment of justice by a Being capable of achieving it can help them to persist in following this rule, belief in Providence and immortality are practically justified. This view is not liable to the criticisms that Kant himself brought against theological ethics. The very use of the word 'hope' (in the *Critique of Pure Reason*)[85] suggests that practical belief is not intended to be unduly assertive.

X. CONCLUSION

According to Kant, then, the various rules of morality are based upon a Moral Law that is pure and *a priori*. It is pure in that it does not contain concepts borrowed from experience of the world and based upon natural inclinations, and it is *a priori* in that it is necessarily valid always and for everyone. The Categorical Imperative gives expression to this Law by indicating its applicability to all persons, its equal recognition of all persons and its free acknowledgment by all persons. It is not in itself a prescription for particular actions, but violations of particular moral rules can be shown to go against it. The cheat and the misanthrope act on principles that could not be applied to all persons, do not recognise all persons as ends in themselves and could not be freely acknowledged by all persons as rules it would be reasonable for them all to conform to. The *a priori* character of the Moral Law is contrasted by Kant with the empirical character of the rules for obtaining happiness. These are learned from experience and do not lay an inescapable obligation upon everyone. If I get my pleasures in different ways from you I need not follow the rules that you follow in order to get yours. We find the rules for happy living by trial and error, and it would be absurd to stick to them when they no longer serve their purpose. They are therefore subject to change as men change and the world changes. The fundamentally non-moral way of regarding human behaviour is that of finding out how things are and what men want and of so adjusting men's actions that their wants and the possibilities which the facts allow are matched with one another. On this basis, rules of behaviour would be reached by way of generalisation and in the light of given desires. But according to Kant, we approach the situation which the conjunction of wants and circumstances has given rise to, with 'a compass in hand', the principle of 'universal legislation'. This cannot be derived from the wants and circumstances, but is, in so far as we are rational, a rule which guides us as we impose our will on them. When Kant says that the Moral Law is *a priori* he does not mean only that it is prescribed by us for all of us – although this is part of what he means – but also that it would be unreasonable not to do so. Furthermore, no *other* principle could replace it. Prescribing a principle of cheating or of maleficence would not be prescribing an *a priori* moral principle. Some, at any rate, of the basic rules of traditional morality are essential ingredients of any rational moral code.

It may be objected that Kant rather negligently groups together selfish concern for one's own happiness and sympathetic concern for the happiness of mankind, and supposes that they both involve hypothetical rather than categorical imperatives. Do not Utilitarians argue that the supreme principle of morality is the promotion of the happiness of all, and that this is something that everyone except idiots and psychopaths has a concern for? Does not Kant reject a morality of sentiment partly because he seems to believe that all desires are selfish and hence that only Counsels of Prudence could result from basing morality on the feelings? The Kantian answer would be that sympathetic feeling, limited as it is both in intensity and extent, would form a most precarious basis for beneficence. Why, apart from prudence, should we then refrain from injuring those whom we do not love or like? If, as the Roman principle has it, we ought not to injure anyone, it is not relevant that we like or dislike them. Either the Utilitarian principle is a specification of the Categorical Imperative after all, or else it is based on feelings which not everyone possesses and no one can be blamed for not having. Unsympathetic men can keep promises and help other people, and psychopaths cannot rightly be excused their cruelty merely on the ground that they dislike their fellow men.

The view that the Moral Law is *a priori* is linked with the Principle of Autonomy. If morality were based entirely on examples we should be drawn towards it by the attractive force of good men and good deeds. But we can only regard these men and deeds as good because we know in general how they ought to act and what ought to be done. If this were not so, we should depend upon our feelings and experiences for our standards of conduct, and might as well be attracted by villains – as intellectually or aesthetically we might be and often are – as by honest men. If the fundamental notion of morality were goodness, morality would depend upon its attractive power. But if duty is fundamental to morality, rules of action take logical precedence over attraction and repulsion. Rules of action enforced by others cannot be a basis for morality, which must depend upon rules of action acknowledged by persons as applicable to them all. Morality is inconsistent, on Kantian principles, both with an unthinking immersion in a fraternal community and with an obstinate refusal to conform with others. Irrational conformity and irrational nonconformity are equally unacceptable. Neither adjustment to nor rejection of established custom is morally requisite, but rather a willing adoption of rules which everyone recognises to be reasonable, and adherence to them in the face of all impulses to the contrary.

We saw that Kant believed that there is no need of science and philosophy to know how to be honest and good. He thought that the Moral Law is plain to all, and that morality is in danger when obvious duties are questioned, doubted, disputed or explained away. If the rightness of actions depended upon consequences, following the rules of morality might lead to the doing of what is wrong. But if Kant is right and consequences are irrelevant the willing performance of duty can never be wrong. As far as I know Kant does not make the point, but to the extent that the maximising of happiness, whether individual or collective, is a matter of research and expertise, there *is* need of science to know how to be good. If circumstances change and rules have to be modified or to be made more complex, experts would be needed to transmit the new discoveries to the people at large, since many of them might not understand the reasons for the change, and would therefore have to follow the authority of the experts instead of acting as autonomous persons. Kant, like Rousseau, believed that uneducated men of ordinary intelligence can achieve virtue and act freely in doing so. It is less likely that such men could freely co-operate in maximising happiness in a world in which the conditions for obtaining it are constantly being changed.

From Schopenhauer onwards Kant has been accused of advocating a morality of blind obedience to the commands of duty – a morality of rigid adherence to uncriticised orders. But Kant's insistence on the Principle of Autonomy hardly accords with this. It is true that Kant thinks that those who do wrong could have refrained from doing so. But it is a condition of doing wrong that the wrongdoer is rational and therefore free. On Kant's view human beings are not slaves to their heredity and environment. Their humanity and rationality just are their ability to act freely in spite of causal influences upon them. People who are ready to be argued out of honesty and benevolence and into cruelty by inquisitors of any sort abandon their autonomy and allow themselves to do what they must know is wrong. Whatever the learned authorities may say, we *know* that men should not be killed for holding religious beliefs that do not harm their fellows. The inquisitors and their supporters, says Kant, violate 'a human duty which is certain in and of itself'.[86] Whatever the arguments are for doing such things, they must be more doubtful than our rational conviction that it is wrong to commit murder. It is rational to uphold such moral principles in the face of arguments and incitements to abandon them. It is not a sign of superior insight to be 'flexible' on such matters, but rather an indication that the rational will has been overcome by unreflective sentiment. The Moral Law is rigid.

This brings us, however, to a gap in Kant's account of morality. He may well be right in saying that duty and the good will are basic to morality, but it is a pity that he has so little to say about ideals of conduct. In the *Groundwork* and the *Critique of Practical Reason* Kant regards the Categorical Imperative as setting limits to the maxims it is permissible for us to adopt and to act on, and he explains his meaning by showing that deceit, malevolence, sloth and other vices could not be made into rules of conduct for everyone. But he does not explore the field of maxims that are not excluded by the test of universal legislation. It is not merely a matter of duty that this man devotes his life to study and this other to the promotion of political reforms, that one pursues a life of personal saintliness and another an ideal of active fidelity to some person or group. Ideals are groups or systems of maxims which provide positive directions to men's lives. The pursuit of them is limited by the Categorical Imperative, so that no ideal is morally acceptable that violates the Moral Law. No one is exempt from the demands of duty, but ideals that do not contravene duty may be chosen, followed and even constructed by one and rejected by another without there being any moral dereliction. Violations of the Moral Law necessarily call for condemnation and sometimes for opposition, and indifference or neutrality in such cases would show that the moral point of view had been abandoned. But we are not called upon to condemn morally departures from an ideal of conduct unless some moral defect is involved. Innocent ideals form the field for toleration.[87] It will be realised that someone who believed that duty is the whole of morality would feel called upon to condemn ideals that he ought to tolerate, and that someone who thought that morality is wholly concerned with ideals might withhold condemnation in circumstances where it ought to be given. Moral fanaticism results from misapprehending the nature of ideals, moral nihilism from failing to recognise the primacy of duty.

Kant then is a rigorist in that he thought that the claims of duty are always absolute against inclinations and against ideals that violate the Moral Law. But he was also a rigorist in that he believed that there can be no exceptions to any basic moral rules. He seems not to have given due weight to situations, much discussed by philosophers since his day, in which one moral claim conflicts with another. Thus he argued that it is wrong to tell a lie even if it appears to be the only way of saving the life of a man who is being pursued by a murderer. It should be noticed that Kant's account of the Categorical Imperative does not require him to adopt this most unplausible view. In discussing this problem Kant says that even if the lie might help the threatened man – and it might not – it would harm humanity as a whole. But if he had applied the Principle of Universal Law to this case he would have asked whether the maxim of telling a lie when an innocent man is threatened in such circumstances could be universalised, and it seems obvious that it could be.[88] In circumstances where one rule of duty conflicts with another, one or the other or both must be broken, and the fact that they are all categorical cannot alter this. Kant, therefore, adopted a false rigorism that is not required by his own principles. His supreme principle of morality does not entail that basic moral rules cannot have exceptions, but only that the permissible exceptions are universalisable maxims.

In conclusion, I should mention that in this brief account of Kant's ethics I have said very little about his general philosophical point of view, but have, as far as possible, discussed his ethical theories in relation to the moral beliefs of ordinary men. We have seen that Kant himself approved of such a course and adopted it himself in the early part of the *Groundwork*. But it should be emphasised that he also interpreted moral principles in terms of his Critical Philosophy as a whole, so that a full discussion of his ethics would have to be carried out in this context.

NOTES

The page references are to the page of the relevant volume of the Prussian Academy of Sciences edition, as these page numbers are usually printed in the margins of twentieth-century editions and translations. The translations are often my own.

1. *Religion within the Bounds of Reason Alone* (1793) book IV, part II. General Observation. Cf. *MM* 436, 'Kneeling down or grovelling on the ground, even to express your reverence for heavenly things, is contrary to human dignity.'
2. *CPrR*, book II, chapter 2.
3. *CPR* A XI.
4. *Prolegomena to any Future Metaphysic* (1783), Introduction.
5. *CPR* A807. Kant's phrase 'acts and omissions' (*Tun und Lassen*), frequent in his writings, is possibly a reminiscence of Wolff's title: *Vernünftige Gedanken von der Menschen Tun und Lassen zur Beförderung ihrer Glückseligkeit* (1720) – 'Rational Thoughts on the Acts and Omissions of Men with a View to the Promotion of their Happiness'.
6. *G* 405.
7. *G* 393.
8. *G* 404.
9. *G* 394–7.
10. *G* 389.
11. *G* 397.
12. *Principia Ethica*, § 94.
13. *G* 399.
14. *MM* 402.
15. *CPrR* 118.
16. *G* 397.
17. H. J. Paton, *The Categorical Imperative*, p. 54. Professor Paton also

says that ' . . . although it is admirable to act for love of another, the man who needs the influence of a good woman to keep him straight may not be a bad fellow, but he does not inspire us with respect'. See also H. J. Paton, *Kant on Friendship.*

18. *G* 401.

19. *CPrR* 76–7.

20. *G* 402, 403.

21. *G* 404.

22. *G* 414.

23. *G* 434.

24. *G* 413.

25. *G* 415–16.

26. L. W. Beck, *A Commentary on Kant's Critique of Practical Reason,* p. 88, and *Studies in the Philosophy of Kant* (New York, 1965) pp. 177 ff. The point is also made by Leonard Nelson, *System of Ethics,* trans. N. Guterman, pp. 45–6. Nelson's book is an excellent modern development of Kantian ethics.

27. *CPrR* 22. *G* 416.

28. *G* 421. In the *CPrR* it is stated as follows: 'Act so that the maxim of your will can also at the same time be valid as a principle of universal legislation.'

29. *G* 421.

30. *CPrR* 27.

31. *G* 422.

32. *CPrR* 27.

33. *G* 423.

34. Sir David Ross, *Kant's Ethical Theory,* p. 30.

35. W. H. Walsh, *Hegelian Ethics* (1969) p. 22. Walsh here refers to Hegel's *Philosophy of Right.* The article from which I have quoted was used by F. H. Bradley in *Ethical Studies* (1876), where he says that Kant's system of moral philosophy 'has been annihilated by Hegel's criticism'. There is an excellent criticism of Hegel's criticism of Kant by Marcus Singer in his *Generalization in Ethics,* pp. 251–3.

36. *G* 423. The word 'mankind' translates Kant's 'das menschliche Geschlecht', lit. 'the human race'.

37. *On the Basis of Morality,* trans. E. F. J. Payne (Library of Liberal Arts: New York, 1965) p. 89.

38. *The Moral Law* (1948) p. 139.

39. *The Categorical Imperative,* p. 152.

40. *MM* 453. A difficult passage to translate. Compare Mary Gregor's translation in *The Doctrine of Virtue* with that of James Ellington in *The Metaphysical Principles of Virtue.* There is a similar passage in Richard Price's *Review of the Principal Questions in Morals,* 3rd edn (1787)

ch. VII. 'All rational beings ought to have a share in our kind wishes and affections. But we are surrounded with *fellow-men*, beings of the same nature, in the same circumstances, and having the same wants with ourselves: to whom therefore we are in a peculiar manner linked and related, and whose happiness and misery depend very much on our behaviour to them.' Price's moral philosophy is discussed by Dr W. D. Hudson in *Ethical Intuitionism* (1967).

41. Julius Ebbinghaus, 'Interpretation and Misinterpretation of the Categorical Imperative', in *Philosophical Quarterly* (1954) p. 105. Kant's account of the Categorical Imperative is effectively defended by Professor Marcus Singer in *Generalization in Ethics*, ch. IX.

42. 1 Corinthians 13:5.

43. G 394.

44. G 389, 391, 407–8, 411–12.

45. G 402.

46. CPrR 22, 27–8.

47. *The Categorical Imperative*, p. 138.

48. Mancur Olsen Jr, *The Logic of Collective Action* (Cambridge, Mass., 1965) pp. 11 ff. and pp. 60–5.

49. G 403.

50. G 434.

51. G 438.

52. CPrR 30.

53. G 429. The principle is assumed in *CPrR* 87.

54. Marcus Singer, *Generalization in Ethics*, p. 236.

55. Klaus Reich, 'Kant and Greek Ethics', I and II, *Mind* (July and October 1939).

56. G 437–8. Commented upon by Paton, *The Categorical Imperative*, pp. 177–8.

57. G 427–8.

58. *Lectures on Ethics*, p. 51. The translation seems to have gone astray at this point, and I have translated the passage from Kant, *Eine Vorlesung über Ethik*, ed. Paul Menzer (Berlin, 1924). The place in the *Groundwork* where Kant says that the will is author of the law is 431. Paton uses the word 'author' on 440, but Kant does not there use that word, but writes of 'legislating'.

59. MM 227.

60. CPR A802.

61. G 404. Cf. 426 and 442.

62. This article is included in *Kant. On History*, ed. L. W. Beck (Library of Liberal Arts: New York, 1963) pp. 3–10.

63. P. A. Schilpp, *Kant's Pre-Critical Ethics*, 2nd edn, pp. 48 and 81.

64. CPR A316.

65. *CPR* A555. The earlier references in the paragraph are to A444 and A448.

66. *CPrR* 30.

67. *CPrR* 96.

67*a*. In the *Critique of Practical Reason* Kant set out what he called 'categories of freedom' to correspond to the theoretical categories of the *Critique of Pure Reason*. For discussion of this obscure part of the *Critique of Practical Reason* see L. W. Beck, *Commentary*, chapter IX.

68. *Essays on the Active Powers of Man*, essay IV, chapter IV.

69. In *Kant. On History*, ed. L. W. Beck, p. 11.

70. *CPrR* 99.

71. *G* 448.

72. *CPR* A632.

73. *CPR* A316.

74. *CPR* A671.

75. *CPR* A771.

76. *CPR* A327.

77. *G* 418.

78. *CPrR* 124.

79. *CJ* 452.

80. *Religion und Philosophie in Deutschland* (Paris, 1834 and 1852).

81. *Kant's Moral Theology*.

82. *CJ* 459.

83. *CPrR* 110.

84. *CJ* 445–6.

85. *CPR* A805, where Kant discusses the three questions: 'What can I know?', 'What ought I to do?', and 'What may I hope?' The first is theoretical and the second and third practical.

86. *Religion within the Bounds of Reason Alone*, ed. Greene and Silber, p. 175.

87. Nelson, *System of Ethics*, part II.

88. Singer, *Generalization in Ethics*, pp. 226–30.

BIBLIOGRAPHY

I. Texts in English Translation

Critique of Judgment, trans. J. H. Bernard, 2nd edn (1931), and J. C. Meredith (Oxford, vol. 1, 1911, vol. 2, 1928).

Critique of Practical Reason, trans. T. K. Abbott, 6th edn (1909), and L. W. Beck (Chicago, 1949).

Critique of Pure Reason, trans. N. K. Smith (1929).

Groundwork of the Metaphysic of Morals, trans. T. K. Abbott (1926), H. J. Paton, with the title *The Moral Law* (1948), and L. W. Beck (Library of Liberal Arts: New York, 1959).

Lectures on Ethics, trans. Louis Infield (1930).

The Metaphysic of Morals. The translations below are of Part II, which is concerned with ethics. Part I is concerned with the philosophy of law.

> *The Metaphysical Principles of Virtue*, trans. J. Ellington, with an Introduction which gives a lucid account of Kant's moral philosophy as a whole, by Warner Wick (Library of Liberal Arts: New York, 1964).

> *The Doctrine of Virtue*, trans. Mary Gregor (Harper Torchbooks: New York, 1964). An acute and exact translation.

Religion within the Bounds of Reason Alone, trans. with an Introduction and Notes by T. M. Greene and H. H. Hudson, with a new essay, 'The Ethical Significance of Kant's *Religion*', by John R. Silber (Harper Torchbooks: New York and Evanston, 1960). Professor Silber's introduction has a helpful discussion of Kant's views on the will.

II. Books about Kant's Ethics

Beck, L. W., *A Commentary on Kant's Critique of Practical Reason* (Chicago, 1960).

Downie, R. S., and Telfer, E., *Respect for Persons* (1969).

Duncan, A. R. C., *Practical Reason and Morality* (Edinburgh, 1957).

Gregor, Mary, *The Laws of Freedom* (Oxford, 1963). Deals particularly with Kant's discussion of duties to oneself, a topic not dealt with in this book.

Kemp, J. C., *Reason, Action and Morality* (1964) ch. v.

Körner, S., *Kant* (1955) chs. 6 and 7.

——, *Kant's Conception of Freedom* (Dawes Hicks Lecture on Philosophy, British Academy, 1967).

Nelson, Leonard, *System of Ethics*, trans. N. Guterman, Foreword by H. J. Paton, Introduction by Julius Kraft (New Haven, 1956). Based on lectures given in Germany, 1916, 1920, 1924. Not an exposition of Kant, but an independent development of Kantian ethics.

Paton, H. J., *The Categorical Imperative* (1947).

——, *Kant on Friendship* (Dawes Hicks Lecture on Philosophy, British Academy, 1956).

Ross, W. D., *Kant's Ethical Theory* (Oxford, 1954).

Schilpp, P. A., *Kant's Pre-Critical Ethics* (Evanston, 1st edn, 1938, 2nd edn, 1960).

Singer, M. G., *Generalization in Ethics* (1963) chs VIII and IX.

Teale, A. E., *Kantian Ethics* (Oxford, 1951).

Walsh, W. H., *Kant's Moral Theology* (Dawes Hicks Lecture on Philosophy, British Academy, 1963).

Williams, T. C., *The Concept of the Categorical Imperative* (Oxford, 1968).